T0387742

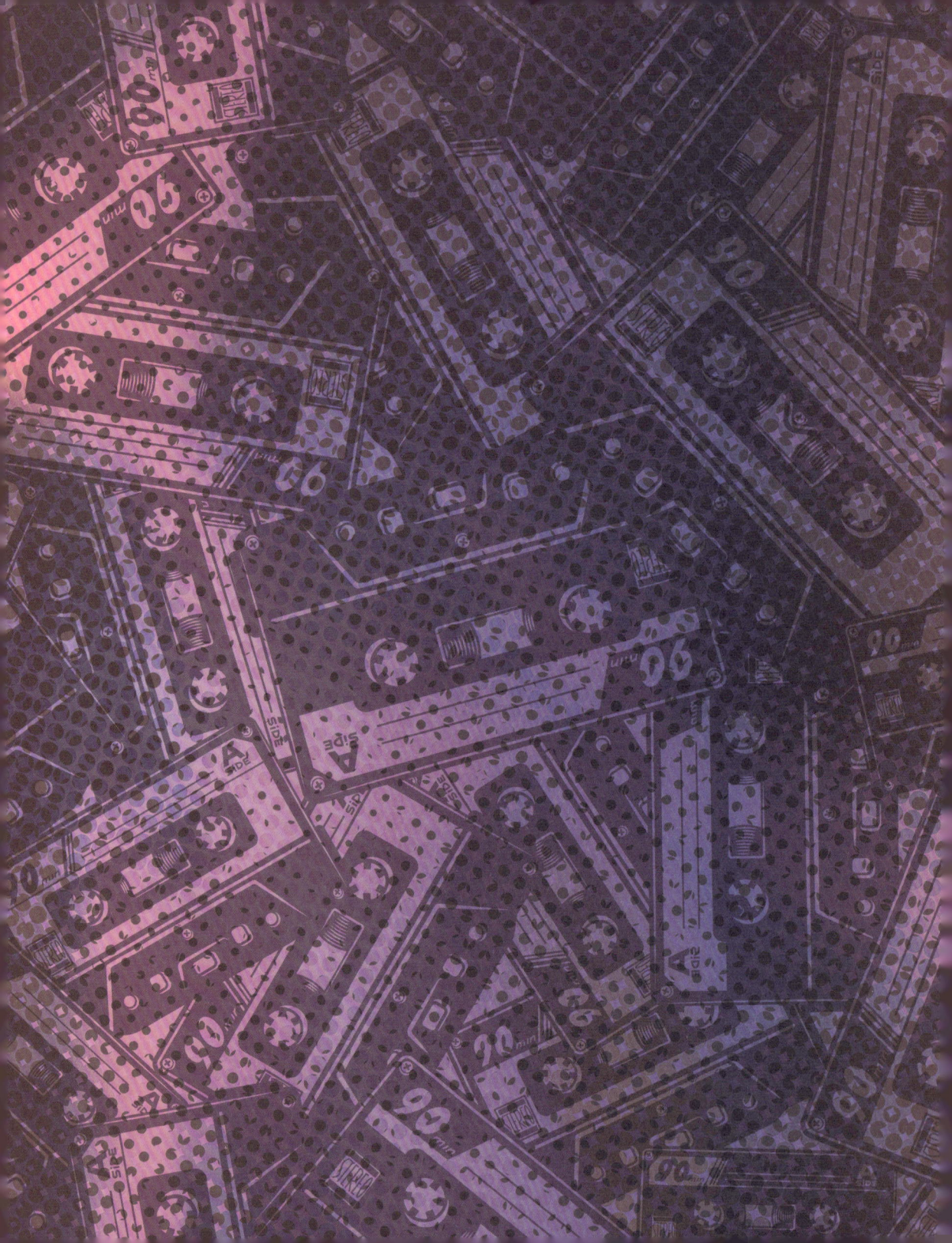

LYRICS & LIBATIONS

TOTALLY '80s COCKTAILS

INSIGHT
EDITIONS

SAN RAFAEL · LOS ANGELES · LONDON

CONTENTS

The '80s

A time when your anonymous phone call could help Robert Stack solve an unsolved mystery. When anthropomorphic fruits and animals sold you underwear and raisins. When commercials were longer than a minute and needlessly dramatic for innate goods like cereal and pantyhose. When you had to pick up the Garfield phone to call your friend's home phone number. When you could bring the first Apple Macintosh computer into your home. When technology was revolutionizing everything from razors to heartburn medicine to (most importantly) music.

Dick Clark once said, "Music is the soundtrack of our lives." And the '80s proved this point like no other decade. The *Thriller* album and music video debut changed the entire landscape of music entertainment. It didn't matter what was being bought or sold, music helped sell it. Music in the '80s was mostly purchased in the form of LPs and cassette tapes—until they were both overtaken by compact discs in 1988.

The '80s weren't always about the money, though. Bob Geldof and Midge Ure wrote the charity song "Do They Know It's Christmas?," which went on to raise $28 million for the famine in Ethiopia. The track included superstars like Bono, David Bowie, Boy George, George Michael, Paul McCartney, and many others. Consequently, this inspired Michael Jackson, Lionel Richie, and Quincy Jones to write and compose "We Are the World" with the help of Cyndi Lauper, Bob Dylan, Stevie Wonder, Tina Turner, Billy Joel, and countless other superstars of the music industry at the time. The single sold 20 million copies globally and raised upward of $10.8 million in aid for Harry Belafonte's organization's efforts to eliminate hunger in Africa and America.

The '80s were a special time unlike any other. These drinks were inspired by the music that made us who we are. Whether you lived through the decade and are ready for a nostalgic trip down memory lane, or you just appreciate this great generation of music, this book is for you. And just like the Hands Across America campaign, this book requires your full participation. We hope you get that body bumping and the drinks flowing.

CHEERS!

MIXERS

Many of us of a certain age got our first impression of bartending from watching *Cocktail* a few dozen times, but mixing drinks isn't about showmanship. The real flair comes from the quality of the drink ingredients. Homemade grenadine, custom syrups, and maybe a drop or two of bartender's saline . . . Nothing elevates a drink like handmade mixers, not even Tom Cruise's biceps in the '80s (talk about top guns!). Sure, you may not be spitting rhymes or twirling bottles around like they're batons, but your drinks will taste *amazing*.

POUR SOME SUGAR ON ME

This syrup will boost the sweetness of any cocktail without changing the overall flavor because, sometimes, you just gotta pour some sugar on it.

1 cup granulated sugar

1 cup water

YIELD: 12 TO 18 USES

1. Add the sugar and water to a small saucepan over medium heat.

2. Stir until the sugar has fully dissolved.

3. Allow syrup to cool, then transfer to a sealable glass container.

4. Store in the refrigerator for up to 4 weeks.

SWEET DREAMS (ARE MADE OF THIS)

You can travel the world and the seven seas, but you won't beat the fruity, sweet, and tart flavor of homemade grenadine.

1 cup pomegranate juice

1 cup granulated sugar

2 teaspoons lemon juice

1 or 2 dashes orange flower water (optional)

YIELD: 12 TO 18 USES

1. In a medium saucepan, combine the pomegranate juice, sugar, and lemon juice.

2. Bring the mixture to a slow boil over medium heat, stirring constantly, until all of the sugar has dissolved.

3. Reduce the heat to low and cover. Simmer for 10 to 15 minutes, stirring occasionally.

4. Allow the mixture to cool, then pour it into a small jar or glass bottle with a tight-sealing lid.

5. Add the orange flower water (if using) and seal the container. Give it a couple shakes.

6. Store in the refrigerator for up to 4 weeks.

Goo Goo Muck

This sultry spiced syrup, with its subtle heat, will unleash the monster in any drink and have you howling at the moon.

1 cup turbinado or demerara sugar

1 cup water

1 tablespoon allspice berries

2 cinnamon sticks

1 dried guajillo or ancho chile pepper (optional)

1-inch fresh ginger slice

1 split vanilla bean or 1 teaspoon vanilla extract

YIELD: 12 TO 18 USES

1. In a small saucepan, combine the turbinado sugar, water, allspice, cinnamon, guajillo pepper (if using), ginger, and vanilla bean and bring to a boil over medium heat, stirring frequently until the sugar has dissolved completely.

2. Once boiling, reduce the heat to low and simmer for 10 to 15 minutes.

3. Remove the pan from the heat and allow the liquid to cool completely before straining out the solids.

4. Store in a sealable container (like a glass bottle) in the refrigerator for up to 4 weeks.

Golden Brown

Although we're pretty sure this isn't the same kind of golden brown as the song, our brown sugar syrup will add rich caramel-toffee notes to your drink. You may even hear that totally rad harpsichord riff as you sip!

1 cup light brown sugar

1 cup water

1 split vanilla bean or 1 teaspoon vanilla extract

1 cinnamon stick (optional)

YIELD: 12 TO 18 USES

1. In a small saucepan, combine the brown sugar, water, vanilla, and cinnamon stick (if using) over medium heat.

2. Simmer, stirring frequently, until the sugar has completely dissolved, about 10 minutes.

3. Remove the syrup from the heat and let it cool to room temperature.

4. Transfer to a sealable airtight container (such as a mason jar) and store in the refrigerator for up to 4 weeks.

MILLI VANILLI

Girl, you know it's true: Vanilla deserves its place as the world's favorite flavor. Milli Vanilli syrup will add some of that sweet, subtle vanilla flavor we all know and love to your drink.

1 cup water

1 cup granulated sugar

2 vanilla pods, split

1 tablespoon vanilla bean paste or vanilla extract

YIELD: 12 TO 18 USES

1. In a small saucepan, combine the water, sugar, and vanilla pods and bring to a boil over medium heat, stirring frequently, until the sugar has dissolved completely.

2. Once boiling, reduce the heat to low and simmer for 5 to 10 minutes.

3. Remove the pan from the heat and allow the liquid to cool completely. Then remove the vanilla pods and stir in the vanilla paste.

4. Store in a sealable container (such as a glass bottle) in the refrigerator for up to 4 weeks.

SMOOTH OPERATOR

There are few things as sophisticated as Sade Adu's vocals or Stuart Matthewman's tenor sax, but this smooth operator comes pretty close. Use it to seamlessly inject the warm, golden flavor of honey into any drink.

1 cup honey

1 cup water

YIELD: 12 TO 18 USES

1. In a small saucepan, combine the honey and water over medium heat.

2. Stir frequently until the honey has fully dissolved.

3. Allow the syrup to cool, then transfer to a sealable airtight container.

4. Store in the refrigerator for up to 4 weeks.

WHEN DOVES CRY

Dig, if you will, a salty solution— presumably not unlike dove tears. Do doves even have tear ducts? We don't know. We do know that when added in small amounts to a drink, bartender's saline makes those citrus and acidic notes SOAR.

1 tablespoon sea salt

⅓ cup warm purified water

YIELD: 16 TO 22 USES

1. In a small bowl, combine the salt and warm water and stir until the salt has fully dissolved.

2. Transfer to a storage container, ideally a small glass dropper bottle.

3. Store in a cool, dark place indefinitely.

ADDICTED TO SHRUB

Put on your black dress, red lipstick, and vague expression—you're about to get addicted to shrub. Shrubs, also known as drinking vinegars, are a combination of fruit, sugar, and vinegar and are a great way to add some bite to nonalcoholic drinks or a little extra tartness to a cocktail.

1 pound strawberries, chopped small

¾ cup granulated sugar

½ cup champagne vinegar or white balsamic vinegar

YIELD: 10 TO 16 USES

1. Put the chopped strawberries and sugar in a large gallon zip-top bag. Seal and shake the bag to coat the strawberries.

2. Let rest at room temperature for 24 hours. The strawberries will release a lot of liquid, so make sure the bag is sealed tight to prevent leaks. It may also be useful to put it on a rimmed baking tray or similar, just in case.

3. Strain the strawberries from the liquid into a large measuring cup or a small mixing bowl. Stir in the vinegar until well combined.

4. Transfer the shrub to a sealable container, such as a mason jar or syrup dispenser. Store in the refrigerator for up to 4 weeks. Use in cocktails as directed or mix one part shrub with three parts sparkling water.

HURTS SO GOOD

Just a few drops of this super-spicy tincture will make your cocktails hurt so good, you might change your last name to Cougar.

1 or 2 fresh habanero peppers

1 dried guajillo or ancho chile

½ cup 100-proof vodka

YIELD: 12 TO 18 USES

1. Using gloves and a sharp knife, remove the stem, pith, and seeds from the chile peppers.

2. Put the seeded chile peppers and vodka in a blender.

3. Pulse until the chiles are mostly pulverized but not puréed.

4. Transfer to a sealable glass storage container.

5. Let infuse for 2 to 3 days, shaking container four to six times a day to agitate.

6. Strain into separate storage container, ideally a glass dropper bottle.

7. Store in a cool, dark place for up to 6 months.

TIPS & TECHNIQUES

If you don't know the first thing about mixology, that's OK. We got you! Think of us like the Mr. Miyagi of mixed drinks. With these basic tips and techniques, you'll be sure to impress your friends. Well, maybe just your mom and your dog, but who's judging? Not us! You got this, champ. So, queue up "The Moment of Truth" by Survivor, we're about to have a training montage, '80s style!

MORE BOUNCE TO THE OUNCE

Cocktail measurements are usually made in fluid ounces using a specialized bartending tool called a jigger. Here's a quick rundown to help you get more bounce to the ounce!

WHAT IS A JIGGER?
A jigger is a bartending tool used to measure alcohol accurately and consistently. A standard jigger features two cups, one larger and one smaller, joined in an hourglass shape. The larger cup typically holds 1.5 ounces, or one "jigger." The smaller cup typically holds 0.75 ounce, or one-half jigger, also known as a "pony" shot. Keep in mind, there is some variation in cup size between the different styles of jiggers, so make sure you know the measurements of your instrument.

ALTERNATIVES
We highly recommend using a jigger when making your cocktails, but you can get away with using other common measuring tools. The key here is consistency. Here's a simple chart to help!

3 ounces (or a double shot) = 6 tablespoons

2 ounces = ¼ cup or 4 tablespoons

1.5 ounces (or 1 jigger) = 3 tablespoons

1 ounce = 2 tablespoons

0.75 ounce (or a pony shot) = 1½ tablespoons

0.5 ounce = 1 tablespoon

0.25 ounce = ½ tablespoon

1 barspoon = 1 teaspoon

MELT WITH YOU

Although most drinks will call for standard ice cubes, some drinks work better with different kinds of ice. This guide will help the ice melt with you, not against you.

WHY ICE MATTERS
The type of ice used in cocktails can change the texture, dilution, and overall taste of a drink. Here are four basic ice types and how they will impact your drink.

STANDARD
Standard-size ice cubes are about 1 inch or 1.25 inches. This is the ice that comes in most ice trays and ice makers. These versatile ice cubes won't melt too fast or too slow and will work great in most cocktails. When using standard ice, add the ice to fill to the top after the drink has been poured—unless the drink is layered or the recipe instructions say otherwise.

CRUSHED AND PEBBLE
Crushed and pebble ice is perfect for strong drinks that could use a little extra dilution. If you don't have an ice machine that makes crushed/pebble ice, you can always make it yourself. Just toss your standard ice cubes in a blender with a little water, pulse, and then strain the excess water before adding the ice to

your glass. Generally, crushed ice should fill the entire serving glass. Using too little crushed ice will actually cause more dilution because the ice will melt too quickly.

LARGE
Large ice cubes are at least 2 inches long and are best for spirit-forward drinks that will be sipped slowly. Because of their large surface area, these big cubes will dilute the drink much more slowly than standard ice cubes.

SHAPED
Ice doesn't always come in cubes. Ice spheres are a popular choice thanks to their slower melt rate and attractive appearance, doubling as a stunning garnish. For highball cocktails, the long, sleek Collins spears are an ideal choice. There are also fun shapes like roses, skulls, and diamonds that add a little extra personality to any drink.

FRANKIE SAYS
KNOW YOUR GLASS

Don't know what kind of glass to use? Relax! We've got you covered. We'll give individual glassware suggestions for each drink in this book, but here's a quick overview to get you acquainted.

MARTINI GLASSES & COUPES
The martini glass makes for a classic, stylish presentation, and its long stem prevents your body heat from warming the drink. Although originally meant to serve champagne, coupes are a similar shape and have become a popular alternative to the martini glass.

COLLINS & HIGHBALL
These tall and slender glasses are ideal for fizzy drinks, as their shape keeps beverages carbonated longer.

SHOT GLASS
Shot glasses only contain a couple ounces of liquid. Drinks served in a shot glass are typically meant to be taken in one swig.

ROCKS AND LOWBALL
Primarily used for serving spirit-forward drinks with few mixers, these glasses are short, stout, and have a thick bottom.

MARGARITA GLASSES
A variation on the coupe, the margarita glass's large rim hosts plenty of surface area, making it ideal for cocktails with a flavored rim.

CHAMPAGNE FLUTES & TULIPS
These glasses were designed for serving drinks that contain sparkling wine. The flute keeps the bubbles longer, whereas the tulip shape allows the drink to aerate and release more aroma.

WINE & BEER GLASSES
Sometimes, there's no need to fix what ain't broke. Wineglasses are perfect for wine-based cocktails like sangria; beer glasses will do just fine for drinks like shandies, which are mixed with beer.

SPECIALTY
A very special drink requires a very special vessel. For instance, copper mugs are used for serving mules because the metal keeps the drink cold. A sour glass, also known as a Delmonico glass, is ideal for sour cocktails, as it allows plenty of room for the luscious foamy top. And tiki glasses? Well, they're just for that island vibe.

You Shook Me All Night Long

Although we all surely want American thighs (whatever that means), it's OK for a good home bartender to skip leg day. Shaking is all in the arms!

WHAT IS SHAKING A COCKTAIL?
It's the act of adding ingredients to a cocktail shaker (or other makeshift cocktail-shaking vessel), with or without ice, and agitating the ingredients by shaking vigorously. In a pinch, you can substitute a shaker for a stainless-steel travel mug.

WHY SHAKE?
Shaking a cocktail achieves a few things: It chills, aerates, and dilutes the drink. Dilution sounds like a bad thing, but it actually helps the ingredients blend together, creating a smoother and more cohesive drink. Shaking is absolutely necessary in drinks that contain egg whites—the agitation develops the frothy texture as the egg whites react to the acidity in the drink.

HOW TO SHAKE A COCKTAIL
After adding the ingredients, place one hand on the bottom of the shaker and one on top of the lid. Make sure your grip is firm enough to ensure that your lid and ice cubes won't fly away like a flock of seagulls. Shake vigorously in a horizontal motion over your shoulder. The time you need to spend shaking will depend on the specific cocktail, but most of the time it will be 10 to 15 seconds, or just until the shaker frosts up.

DRY SHAKING
Most of the time, cocktails are shaken with ice to chill and dilute the drink (also called "wet shaking"). Cocktails that include egg whites, however, will need to be shaken without ice first ("dry shaking"). This results in a rich, velvety mouthfeel and a thick foam layer that rests on top of the drink.

TIPS
You want to use standard or large ice cubes for shaking—never crushed ice, as it melts too quickly and causes the drink to become watery.

We Built This City

We built this city on rock and roll . . . and maybe some vodka. The alternative to stirring and shaking is called building, so let's start at the ground floor.

WHAT IS BUILDING A COCKTAIL?
Building essentially means adding the drink ingredients directly to the serving glass in a specific order.

WHY BUILD?
If a drink contains bubbles or layers, it's usually better to build. Sometimes you'll want to shake or stir the individual layers, but after the carbonated ingredients have been added to the drink, you don't want to mess with it too much.

HOW TO BUILD
How to build a drink will vary from drink to drink, so there's no standard way to do it; you'll just want to follow the order given in the recipe. Generally, for drinks with carbonated ingredients, the noncarbonated ingredients go in first, then the carbonated ingredients are added to fill. For layered drinks, typically the layers with the most density—usually the sweetest and least alcoholic ingredients—will go in first. More on layering later.

TIPS
Building is the simplest of the cocktail-making techniques, but there can be pitfalls. You will need to be very mindful of the order as written in the recipe, because adding the ingredients in the wrong order could weaken the flavors or appearance of your drink.

HEAD OVER HEELS

It's great to be head over heels, but for layering, you're going to want to keep things in order. And once you discover how effortlessly you can layer a drink, you'll find yourself head over heels in love with crafting stunning layered cocktails.

WHY LAYER?
Layering ingredients can add visual appeal to a drink by making the presentation more colorful and dynamic.

THE SCIENCE OF LAYERING
The basic rule is that the heaviest liquids need to be at the bottom. The heaviest liquids also tend to be the sweetest or most sugar dense. There are some exceptions depending on the ingredient, but cocktail layers usually work out like this:

Base Layer: Syrups

Second Layer: Liqueurs

Third Layer: Juices or dairy

Fourth Layer: Spirits

Fifth Layer: Foam (from egg whites or aquafaba) or whipped cream

HOW TO LAYER
The process of layering is easier than it seems. The simple trick for achieving distinct layers is to use a spoon. Ideally, you would use a barspoon, but any small spoon will work. Holding the spoon directly over the base layer, slowly pour the next layer over the spoon, letting the spoon overflow. This should result in the next layer floating on top of the previous one, creating a visual contrast. Continue until you have added all your layers.

TIP
Contrary to the common recommendation to use the back of the spoon, it doesn't tend to make much difference in practice. With smaller cups, such as shot glasses, it is actually much better to hold the spoon facing up.

STIR YOU LIKE A HURRICANE

Ironically, you don't usually stir a Hurricane (the cocktail). We'll tell you why, and how to properly stir a drink, right here.

WHAT IS STIRRING A COCKTAIL?
Stirring is just what it sounds like. In the case of cocktails. When a cocktail is "stirred," it means the ingredients were combined with ice in a separate glass, called a mixing glass, and then strained into the serving glass.

MIXING GLASSES
A mixing glass doesn't have to be anything special; it just needs to have a wide enough opening so that you can give the drink a decent stir. There are mixing glasses designed specifically for this purpose, but a rocks glass will work fine in most cases.

WHY STIR?
A gentler method than shaking, stirring allows for a drink to be chilled without changing its texture or appearance. A common rule is that drinks consisting mostly, or entirely, of spirits, without any fruit juices, should be stirred, not shaken.

HOW TO STIR A COCKTAIL
Ideally, you should chill the mixing glass first. This can be done by placing the glass in the freezer for 10 to 15 minutes. Alternatively, you can add ice water to the glass, stir, and then empty it. Add the drink ingredients and fill the glass two-thirds full with standard ice. Place a spoon (ideally a barspoon) into the mixing glass, such that the back of the spoon sits against the edge of the glass, and then move the spoon around the edge of the glass to rotate the ice. Do this for 20 to 30 seconds, until the ingredients are well chilled, then strain the liquid into the serving glass.

TIPS
Try to be as gentle as possible when stirring a drink. Unlike shaking, the goal of stirring is to cause as little agitation as possible while chilling the beverage.

PUSH IT

All right, sexy people, get ready to work that muddler just right. Ooh, baby baby!

WHAT IS MUDDLING?

Muddling is the act of gently smashing ingredients like herbs, fruits, and spices so that they release their essence into a drink. This technique is an essential part of cocktails like mojitos, juleps, and other drinks that use fresh fruits, herbs, and berries.

WHY MUDDLE?

Muddling helps release the flavors of the herbs or fruits being used.

HOW TO MUDDLE

The easiest way is using a specifically designed tool called a "muddler." However, you can use any long, blunt kitchen instrument, such as the handle of a wooden spoon; you may just have to work slightly harder. Here are the steps for a proper muddle:

Add the ingredients to either a glass with a sturdy base or a cocktail shaker, depending on the recipe.

Gently but firmly push down (real good!) and twist the muddler at the same time.

Repeat this motion five or six times until the ingredients are fragrant and lightly smashed.

TIPS

Be careful not to overmuddle or push too hard, as this can not only damage and bruise your ingredients, causing unpleasant flavors in certain herbs like mint, but can also break the glass and/or hurt your hands. Unlike other Salt-N-Pepa-recommended activities, muddling should only take four or five good pumps.

TAKE MY BREATH AWAY

In the '80s, you'd slab on some blue eyeshadow and spritz yourself in a cloud of Aqua Net before heading out to the mall, probably to buy the *Top Gun* soundtrack at Tape World. Well, '80s-themed cocktails need a touch of that '80s glamor, too. We'll teach you how to make your drinks . . . breathtaking.

WHAT IS A COCKTAIL GARNISH?

A cocktail garnish is an ornamental item added to a drink to give it a more breathtaking appearance. Like ice and glassware, garnishes can also have flavor-enhancing qualities.

WHY GARNISH?

Although garnishing a drink is almost always optional, garnishes can really enhance the drinking experience. Cherries and citrus fruits are popular choices and easy ways to add sweetness and color to a drink. A sprig of mint also adds a visual appeal and an aromatic element. Salt rims look good but also enhance the flavor of citrus-forward drinks. More on rims later!

HOW TO GARNISH

Garnishing is a great opportunity to add your personality to a drink, as there is no right or wrong way to do it. Arrange your garnishes in whatever way feels right and makes you happy!

TIPS

When using a citrus peel or twist, make sure to remove the pith (the white part) of the peel as much as possible. The garnish will both look and taste better, as the pith can impart an overly bitter flavor.

You Spin It Round (Like A Record)

Some of the recipes in this cocktail book call for rimming the serving glass, and to rim, you need to SPIN. Time to spin that glass right round, baby!

WHY RIM?

Like garnishes, rimming a glass enhances the flavor and aesthetic appeal of the drink and, in some cases, it also provides some textural contrast.

HOW TO RIM A GLASS

Rimming a glass is easy and takes less than a minute. Here is a general guideline to help.

Note: Most recipes will only call for a liquid and/or a rimmer. Additional flavorings and food coloring are less common additions.

INGREDIENTS:

1 to 2 tablespoons liquid (such as juice or syrup)

1 to 2 tablespoons rimmer (such as salt and/or sugar)

1 teaspoon other flavorings (such as citrus zest or spices, optional)

1 or 2 drops food coloring (optional)

METHOD:

Pour the liquid into a small shallow bowl.

In a separate small shallow bowl, combine the sugar, salt, food coloring, and/or other flavorings. Stir to mix, if necessary.

Turn the serving glass upside down and dip the rim of the glass into the liquid.

Now dip the moistened rim of the glass into the bowl with the sugar, salt, and/or other flavoring.

Rotate the glass so that the rimmer and flavoring sticks to the moistened rim.

Set the glass aside while you prepare the drink.

The Safety Dance

A wise man once said that you have to take a chance and everything will work out right. But before you start lighting drinks on fire and skipping off to dance around the maypole at the local Ren Faire, make sure to heed these essential safety tips.

BURNIN' FOR YOU: PREVENTING ETERNAL FLAMES

Yes, there are a couple of drinks in this book that involve setting stuff on fire. We *did* start the fire, Billy. It was us. Setting stuff on fire is fun, but before you do it in your home—and especially before you've had too many drinks—make sure you're prepared to put those fires out. Here are some tips:

- **Clear the area:** Ensure that the surrounding surface where you will prepare the drink is free from flammable substances and clutter.

- **Suffocate the flame:** The most efficient way to stop a fire is to suffocate it. You can use a large pot, glass, vase (one that the serving glass can fit completely inside), or fire blanket.

- **Be prepared:** Always have a way to extinguish the fire handy, and a backup, too. For instance, it's smart to keep both a fire blanket and a fire extinguisher nearby.

- **Ensure the fire is out:** Make sure the fire is completely out and the glass is cooled before picking up and enjoying your drink.

- **Avoid drafts:** Make sure there are no drafts or strong air currents that could spread the flame unexpectedly.

BE EGGS-CELLENT TO EACH OTHER

Cocktails in the sour family sometimes call for raw egg whites. Some, like flips and nogs, even call for whole raw eggs. Although the risk of illness from undercooked eggs is very low—the Centers for Disease Control estimates that the risk of an egg being contaminated with salmonella is about 1 in 20,000—there's still a small chance of getting sick. Raw eggs should be avoided entirely by the very young, the very old, and the immunocompromised. Consider egg-white alternatives like aquafaba (chickpea water) and commercial cocktail foamers. For those who can afford to live a little dangerously, here are some tips to mitigate the risks:

- **Use pasteurized eggs and/or egg whites:** These are treated to kill bacteria without cooking the egg.

- **Refrigerate eggs:** Don't leave eggs out of the refrigerator for more than 2 hours.

- **Check for cracks:** Don't use eggs with cracked shells.

- **Inspect freshness:** Use eggs before their expiration date. When in doubt, perform a freshness test by placing the egg in water—fresh eggs will sink, whereas older ones will float.

- **Sanitize equipment:** Thoroughly wash and sanitize all your equipment after working with eggs.

- **Use safe handling practices:** Always wash your hands before and after handling raw eggs.

FUNKY COLD MEDICAL EMERGENCY

Using dry ice is a funky little trick that can super-chill your drink and create a rad misty effect as the carbon dioxide transitions from a solid to a gas. However, dry ice can be dangerous, so it's important to use it with caution. Here are some tips to keep safe:

- **Handle with tongs:** Never handle dry ice directly. Always use tongs, as frostbite can occur in a matter of seconds.

- **Wear protective gear:** It doesn't hurt to wear protective gear, such as thick gloves and glasses or goggles, when working with dry ice.

- **Avoid ingestion:** Never ingest any dry ice. Even a small amount can cause serious frostbite burns inside the body. Ensure the dry ice has evaporated completely before taking the first sip.

- **Ensure ventilation:** Always use dry ice in a well-ventilated area, as the fumes can cause asphyxiation.

- **Use a barrier:** Consider using a barrier around the dry ice, like a tea infuser, before putting it into the drink to prevent accidental ingestion.

- **Monitor the amount:** Use small pieces of dry ice to control the intensity of the effect and to ensure quicker dissipation.

- **Educate guests:** Inform your guests about the presence of dry ice in their drinks and the associated safety precautions.

HEAVY METAL, NOT HEAVY MACHINERY

Heavy metal and cocktails can make for an unforgettable night, but combining alcohol with heavy machinery (like a car) is a recipe for disaster. Here are some essential tips to keep your night fun and incident-free:

- **Designate a driver early:** Before the first drink is mixed, establish a designated driver who will stay sober for the evening.

- **Pace yourself:** Have no more than one drink per hour. This helps your body process the alcohol more efficiently and keeps you from getting too intoxicated too quickly.

- **Stay hydrated and nourished:** Alternate alcoholic drinks with nonalcoholic beverages like water or juice. Eating snacks throughout the evening will also help slow the absorption of alcohol.

- **Allow time to sober up:** Give yourself at least three hours to sober up before considering driving or operating any heavy machinery. Better yet, if you're in a safe environment, sleep it off first.

- **Know your limits:** Pay attention to how you're feeling and recognize when it's time to stop. Everyone's tolerance is different, and it's good to know your own.

- **The buddy system:** Keep an eye on your friends and make sure everyone is safe. Sometimes, it's easier to recognize when someone else needs to slow down or stop drinking.

- **Use a ride-sharing service:** If no one can be a designated driver, plan to use a ride-sharing service or a taxi to get home safely. See, some things have improved since the '80s! Obviously not music, though.

BACK IN BLACK

Activated charcoal is a great ingredient for adding a deep black color to your drinks, making them 100% more badass. However, consuming large amounts of it can interfere with the absorption of medications. Always be mindful of your guests' health and medication needs when incorporating this ingredient into your drinks.

CBD PSA:

I LEARNED IT BY WATCHING YOU!

Our collective attitude toward marijuana (in all its forms) has changed somewhat since the '80s. In areas where recreational use is legal, CBD can be an intriguing cocktail ingredient. However, as with anything, it's important to make informed choices.

Start Small: When using CBD in cocktails, start with a small dose to assess tolerance.

Find a Reputable Source: Ensure you're using high-quality CBD from a reputable and trusted source.

Amplifying Effects: Be aware that CBD and alcohol can enhance each other's effects, leading to increased drowsiness or impairment.

Avoiding Hazards: Avoid driving or operating heavy machinery after consuming CBD-infused drinks.

Ask a Pro: Consult a healthcare professional before consumption if you have health conditions or take medications that might be affected by CBD use.

COULD YOU BE LOVED

Bob Marley and the Wailers: *Uprising*

Far more than just the guy on a poster on your college roommate's wall, Bob Marley was a revolutionary, a prophet, and a true legend who could jump from anthems of love and hope right into grounded, stark cries for justice. Reggae is a genre with a wide variety of artists and sounds, but Bob Marley and the Wailers is still the starting point for anyone with an interest in Jamaican music. His face may be on lunchboxes and tea cans, but nothing can take away what he stood for and against.

1½ ounces Jamaican rum

1½ ounces spiced rum

3 ounces orange pineapple juice

¾ ounce Sweet Dreams (page 6) or other grenadine

¾ ounce lime juice

2 or 3 dashes Jamaican bitters, jerk bitters, or other Caribbean spiced bitters

2 to 3 ounces bold ginger beer, chilled

GARNISH

Pineapple slices

Lime wheels

Maraschino cherries

1. In a cocktail shaker filled with ice, add the Jamaican rum, spiced rum, pineapple juice, Sweet Dreams, lime juice, and bitters.

2. Shake vigorously for 20 to 25 seconds until well chilled and foamy.

3. Strain into the serving glass.

4. Add standard ice until the glass is two-thirds full.

5. Top with ginger beer.

6. Garnish with pineapple slices, lime wheels, and maraschino cherries.

FUN FACTS: This was the first reggae song to get prominent airplay on major American radio stations, played first by Frankie Crocker on the New York radio station WBLS.

GLASS: DELMONICO/SOUR, COUPE, OR DOUBLE ROCKS
ICE: NONE OR 1 LARGE • **SERVES:** 1

LOVE WILL TEAR US APART

Joy Division

Somehow, Joy Division is a band that might be known more for their album art appearing on T-shirts than for their brief musical career. Beyond the stark radio waves from their debut *Unknown Pleasures*, though, the influence of the Manchester act can be heard in basically any band that's ever dressed in all black. You can hear a little of Ian Curtis and company in acts from The Cure to Deftones, Depeche Mode to Interpol. This drink is a lot like love. It's sweet, sour, and bitter. Luckily, the only things tearing apart in this drink are the eggs, so go and love to your heart's content.

2 ounces rye whiskey

1 ounce lemon juice

¾ ounce coffee liqueur or crème de cassis

¼ ounce Pour Some Sugar on Me (page 6) or other simple syrup

2 or 3 dashes coffee bitters or aromatic bitters

2 or 3 drops When Doves Cry (page 8) or other saline

1 egg white or 2 tablespoons aquafaba

GARNISH

Cocktail cherries

Cocktail skewer

1. In a cocktail shaker, combine the whiskey, lemon juice, coffee liqueur, Pour Some Sugar on Me, bitters, When Doves Cry, and egg white.

2. Shake for 25 to 35 seconds until foamy.

3. Fill the shaker with ice.

4. Shake for 10 to 15 seconds until well chilled.

5. Strain into the serving glass.

6. Garnish with skewered cocktail cherries.

FUN FACTS: This song was written as a more cynical response to "Love Will Keep Us Together" by Captain & Tennille.

I'M COMING OUT

Diana Ross: *Diana*

On one fateful night in 1979, Rock & Roll Hall of Famer Nile Rodgers went to an underground trans nightclub in New York City. It was in the bathroom that Rodgers met a gaggle of Diana Ross impersonators and a lightbulb went off in his head. Behold: the birth of one of the most important gay anthems of any generation. Take the time to pour one out for the LGBTQIA+ brothers, sisters, and allies who fought long and hard for the gays of today to be able to say . . . I'm coming out! Or whatever cool equivalent the kids are saying today. The point is: slay.

¼ ounce Sweet Dreams (page 6) or other grenadine

2 ounces tequila blanco

2 ounces guava juice, chilled

½ ounce lime juice

1 ounce peach nectar, chilled

2 ounces club soda, chilled

GARNISH

Mint sprigs

Lime wheels

Maraschino cherries

1. Pour the Sweet Dreams into the bottom of the glass.

2. Fill the glass two-thirds full with standard ice.

3. In a cocktail shaker filled with ice, add the tequila, guava juice, and lime juice.

4. Shake for 10 to 15 seconds until well chilled.

5. Strain into the serving glass.

6. Give the drink a stir to slightly blend the Sweet Dreams and create a gradient.

7. Top with peach nectar, followed by the club soda.

8. Garnish with mint sprigs, lime wheels, and cherries.

FUN FACTS: The trombone solo was performed by Meco Monardo, best known for his 1977 space disco version of the Star Wars theme from his album *Star Wars and Other Galactic Funk*.

23

GLASS: HURRICANE, MARGARITA, SCHOONER, OR MILKSHAKE • **ICE:** NONE • **SERVES:** 2

Whip It

Devo: *Freedom of Choice*

Devo's attempts to subvert commercialism with songs like "Whip It" ironically made them as much a part of the American consumer experience as the microplastics coursing in our blood. You might be humming off a version of the song from a mop commercial right now, but "Whip It" isn't just a weird track by Ohio guys with red flower pots on their heads: this hyperliterate riff on limericks and poems from recluse author Thomas Pynchon's *Gravity's Rainbow* also serves as a tribute of sorts to Jimmy Carter, who was being ousted from the White House by '80s uber-villain Ronald Reagan. Could they have guessed their megahit would end up pairing so well with whipped cream commercials?

WHIPPED CREAM

1 cup heavy cream or full-fat coconut milk (from a can), chilled

2 teaspoons granulated sugar

1 teaspoon vanilla extract

WHIPPED LEMONADE

5 ounces citron or whipped vodka

½ cup lemon juice

½ cup sweetened condensed milk or cream of coconut syrup

1½ cups ice cubes

GARNISH

Lemon wheel

Red maraschino cherry

1. Whip the cream and then add to a medium mixing bowl with the sugar and vanilla. Use a hand mixer to whip the cream until soft, but stable, peaks form. Set the whipped cream aside in the fridge for now.

2. In a blender, combine the citron, lemon juice, sweetened condensed milk, ice cubes to taste, and two-thirds of the whipped cream (reserving the rest for the topping).

3. Blend until smooth, about 1 to 2 minutes on high speed.

4. Divide into two serving glasses.

5. Add the remaining whipped cream to a piping bag or a zip-top bag with one corner cut off. Pipe the whipped cream on top of the drinks.

6. Garnish with a lemon wheel and a maraschino cherry and serve!

FUN FACTS: Several journalists consider "Whip It" a foundational song in the development of new wave music, being one of the first major pop hits to heavily incorporate synthesizers and post-punk sensibilities. Music critic Evie Nagy called it a "defining anthem of new wave's rise."

The main riff in "Whip It" is pulled from Roy "The Caruso of Rock" Orbison's 1964 "Oh, Pretty Woman," but with the ending slightly altered.

HIT ME WITH YOUR BEST SHOT

Pat Benatar: *Crimes of Passion*

We don't show enough respect for Pat Benatar. She walked in tight athletic gear so today's yoga-pants-clad moms could run. Now, you don't have to be a real tough cookie to take this shot, but it helps if you are. Hey, we're not all cut from the same purple zebra spandex as Pat Benatar, and we all know that sometimes people don't fight fair. Some of us are soft-cookie-dough kids who just want to enjoy a shot, so put your dukes down and enjoy.

¾ ounce cookie dough whiskey

½ ounce dark crème de cacao

¼ ounce coffee liqueur

Pinch edible luster dust (optional)

1 or 2 drops Hurts So Good (page 9) (optional)

GARNISH

Chocolate frosting or corn syrup, for the rim

Red sprinkles, for the rim

Whipped cream

Cookie crumbles, for sprinkling (optional)

1. Rim the shot glass with chocolate frosting and red sprinkles (see Rimming Guide, page 15).

2. In a cocktail shaker filled with ice, add the whiskey, crème de cacao, coffee liqueur, luster dust (if using), and Hurts So Good (if using).

3. Shake for 10 to 15 seconds until well chilled.

4. Strain into the serving glass.

5. Top with whipped cream and cookie crumbles (if using).

FUN FACTS: Pat won the Grammy Award for Best Female Rock Vocal Performance four years in a row, from 1980 to 1983, and has six platinum albums.

9 TO 5

Dolly Parton: *9 to 5 And Odd Jobs*

This super-fun song is an all-time classic, but it's a little weird to think that the movie it came from has the trio of Jane Fonda, Lily Tomlin, and Dolly herself getting high and plotting to murder their boss. It doesn't matter, though, as Dolly can do no wrong. The movie and song are about busting your keister for an ungrateful boss, so we wanted to keep that spirit—no pun intended—for the drink. It's probably a bad idea to make one of these at the office, but if you're lucky enough to work from home, then you might as well let it rip. Just remember to keep your cocktail glass off-camera during Zoom calls.

1½ ounces Tennessee whiskey or bourbon

1 ounce coffee liqueur

½ ounce Golden Brown (page 7)

3 or 4 dashes pecan bitters

4 to 5 ounces strong, hot coffee

2 ounces heavy cream

GARNISH

Pinch ground cinnamon

1 praline

1. Pour the cold cream into a small mixing bowl. Use a hand mixer to whip the cream until stiff peaks form. Set aside.

2. In the serving glass, combine the whiskey, coffee liqueur, Golden Brown, and pecan bitters and give it a stir.

3. Add the hot coffee, leaving an inch of room for the whipped cream topping.

4. Spoon or pipe the whipped cream on top of the drink. Garnish with ground cinnamon and a praline.

FUN FACTS: Parton wrote this song for the 1980 film of the same name, which was Parton's acting debut. With it, Parton became the second woman to top both the US country singles chart and the *Billboard* Hot 100 with the same single.

GLASS: MARTINI OR COUPE • **ICE:** NONE OR 1 LARGE • **SERVES:** 1

HIGHER PLANE

Al Green: *Higher Plane*

This track is an oddly sexy inclusion for a gospel album, but hey, that's the great contradiction of the Reverend Al. The super-funky bass line and disco strings might have been intended as a theme song for Jesus, but they work just as well for a *Soul Train* line in your living room. This beverage is for the holy rollers. We give you the choice between using Bénédictine and Yellow Chartreuse. It all depends on how much money you want to have left over for when the donation basket comes your way.

1 ounce bourbon

1 ounce Aperol®

1 ounce Bénédictine® or Yellow Chartreuse®

1 ounce lemon juice

3 to 5 dashes aromatic bitters

GARNISH

Lemon peel or a small paper plane

1. In a cocktail shaker filled with standard ice, add the bourbon, Aperol, Bénédictine, lemon juice, and bitters.

2. Shake for 10 to 15 seconds until well chilled.

3. Strain into the serving glass.

4. Garnish with a lemon peel.

FUN FACTS: Speaking of Bénédictine, Chartreuse was perfected by the French chapter of the monastic order in 1605. They called it the "elixir of long life." To that we say: drink and live forever, baby.

RAPTURE

Blondie: *Autoamerican*

No idea who she's talking about with the "man from Mars" line, but Debbie Harry somehow pulled off being a white rapper all the way back in 1981 with what ended up being the first American number-one record to feature rapped lyrics. Take in Harry's lazy, hypnotic rap style while rattling your cocktail shaker until the cold becomes too much. This will give you just enough time to reconsider everything you thought you knew about Debbie Harry. Is she an early rap star? Is she the real Slim Shady? Did Eminem ever party with Basquiat?

1 ounce Cognac or tequila anejo (or do a split base)

1 ounce brandy-based orange liqueur or orange curaçao

½ ounce lemon juice

½ ounce lime juice

¼ ounce agave syrup (optional)

2 or 3 dashes orange bitters

GARNISH

Lemon or lime juice, for the rim

Granulated sugar, for the rim

Orange peel

1. Rim the glass with lemon juice and sugar (see Rimming Guide, page 15).

2. In a cocktail shaker filled with standard ice, add the Cognac, orange liqueur, lemon juice, lime juice, agave syrup (if using), and bitters.

3. Shake for 10 to 15 seconds until well chilled.

4. Strain into the serving glass.

5. Garnish with an orange peel.

FUN FACTS: The music video for "Rapture" became the first rap video ever broadcast on MTV and was part of its original ninety-video rotation. The video featured cameos from Fab 5 Freddy (who is mentioned in the lyrics) and graffiti artists Lee Quiñones and Jean-Michel Basquiat. Basquiat was hired when Grandmaster Flash did not show up to the shoot.

VIENNA

Ultravox: *Vienna*

The only thing that will make this drink better is if you suit up in the leather-daddy outfit that lead singer Midge Ure wore during Ultravox's 1981 televised Christmas performance for the legendary UK show *Top of the Pops*. Go ahead, we'll wait while you run to YouTube to check it out. And if anyone asks, you can just say you're really into drinking coffee cocktails while shopping online for a Harley-Davidson. Your secret is safe with us.

½ cup heavy cream, chilled

½ ounce Milli Vanilli (page 8) or other vanilla syrup

2 shots espresso or 2 ounces very strong coffee

¾ ounce dark chocolate liqueur or dark crème de cacao

½ ounce almond or orange liqueur (optional)

GARNISH

Cocoa powder or chocolate shavings

1. In a medium mixing bowl, combine the cold cream and Milli Vanilli.

2. Use a hand mixer to whip the cream for 2 to 3 minutes or until stiff peaks form.

3. Transfer the whipped cream to a piping bag or a zip-top bag with one corner cut off. Set the whipped cream aside.

4. In the serving glass, pour the espresso, dark chocolate liqueur, and almond liqueur (if using), then stir to combine.

5. Pipe the cream on top of the coffee mixture in the serving glass.

6. Garnish with cocoa powder.

FUN FACTS: **The partially black-and-white video was the first "mini movie" music video. It was directed by Russell Mulcahy, one of the biggest music video directors of the early '80s. Mulcahy directed videos for acts like AC/DC, The Human League, The Sex Pistols, Culture Club, and The Buggles's landmark video for "Video Killed the Radio Star" in 1979. He also directed the 1986 fantasy action film *Highlander*.**

THE DUDE

Quincy Jones: *The Dude*

Who really has the right to be called The Dude? Yes, Jeff Bridges laid claim to abiding in *The Big Lebowski,* but Quincy Jones has twenty-eight Grammys, made "We Are the World" happen, wrote the theme to *Sanford and Son,* produced *The Fresh Prince of Bel Air,* had an essential role in Michael Jackson's success, and is Rashida Jones's dad. We probably don't need to fight about it, but this song is a much better fit for a sweet drink with a touch of hotness than any of Jeff Bridges's country tracks, at least.

2 ounces tequila

2 ounces pineapple juice

1½ ounces raspberry or watermelon pucker

½ ounce yuzu or lime juice

3 or 4 dashes hot sauce (optional)

GARNISH

Chamoy or corn syrup, for the rim

Tajín® or shichimi togarashi, for the rim

Lime wheel

1. Rim the glass with chamoy and Tajín or shichimi togarashi (see Rimming Guide, page 15).

2. In a cocktail shaker filled with ice, add the tequila, pineapple juice, raspberry pucker, yuzu juice, and hot sauce to taste (if using).

3. Shake for 10 to 15 seconds until well chilled.

4. Strain into the serving glass.

5. Garnish with a lime wheel and serve!

UNDER PRESSURE

Queen with David Bowie: *Hot Space*

You know the saying: There *can* be too much of a good thing. And it would seem that when you put two famous vocalists in a room, there might not be one big enough for both of their egos, as evidenced by the tension between Bowie and Mercury during the recording of "Under Pressure." But then again, how can there not be friction when two larger-than-life personalities are essentially competing with each other in the midst of a smash hit? They were just applying pressure.

¼ cup fresh raspberries

4 or 5 basil leaves or large mint leaves

2 ounces red berry vodka or unflavored vodka

½ ounce lemon juice

2 ounces sparkling raspberry seltzer water

2 ounces lemon-lime soda

GARNISH

Fresh raspberries

Basil leaves or mint sprigs

1. In the serving glass, muddle the raspberries and basil until the berries are thoroughly smashed and the basil is fragrant (see Muddling Guide, page 14).

2. Add the vodka and lemon juice and give the drink a stir.

3. Add a Collins spear or standard ice to the glass until it is two-thirds full.

4. Top with raspberry seltzer and lemon-lime soda to taste.

5. Garnish with fresh raspberries and basil leaves.

FUN FACTS: Throughout the '80s, it was trendy for two musical superstars to team up to release a hit single. Other notable combinations included Paul McCartney and Stevie Wonder on "Ebony and Ivory" (page 45), Kenny Rogers and Dolly Parton on "Islands in the Stream," Diana Ross and Lionel Richie on "Endless Love," and Aerosmith and Run-D.M.C. on "Walk This Way." "Under Pressure" was the first time Queen had ever collaborated with another artist.

ONCE IN A LIFETIME

Talking Heads: *Remain in Light*

Hopefully, you enjoy this cocktail in your living room, even if you're not sure how you got there, and not in a shotgun shack, but either way, you'll probably ask yourself, "How did I make this amazing drink? My god, what have I done?" Definitely stay away from the wheel of a large automobile, but feel free to consider how there's water underground and head into the blue again. Same as it ever was, indeed.

2 ounces overproof white rum

¼ ounce blue curaçao (optional)

¾ ounce lime juice

½ ounce Pour Some Sugar on Me (page 6) or other simple syrup

3 or 4 drops When Doves Cry (page 8)

2 or 3 drops grapefruit or other citrus bitters

3 to 4 ounces sparkling mineral water, chilled

GARNISH

Cocktail cherries

1 cocktail skewer

1. In a cocktail shaker filled with standard ice, add the rum, curaçao (if using), lime juice, Pour Some Sugar on Me, When Doves Cry, and bitters.

2. Shake for 10 to 15 seconds until well chilled.

3. Strain into the serving glass.

4. Fill the glass two-thirds full with standard or large ice.

5. Add sparkling mineral water to fill.

6. Garnish with skewered cocktail cherries.

FUN FACTS: The video was choreographed by Toni Basil (known for her hit single "Mickey").

1982

THRILLER

Michael Jackson: *Thriller*

Yes, this is the title track of an album that was number one for more than a year. Yes, it's still the number-one-selling album of all time worldwide, having sold around 70 million copies. But let's also recognize that the true accomplishment of this song was creating an instant Halloween classic and nabbing Vincent Price a spot on the charts. I mean, if you're making a playlist for a boo bash, you put "Thriller" on there first. What else comes even close? "Monster Mash"? Maybe a Misfits song? "Werewolf Bar Mitzvah"?

¾ ounce whiskey or bourbon

1 ounce almond liqueur

1½ ounces tart cherry juice

¾ ounce lemon juice

½ ounce Goo Goo Muck (page 7)

3 or 4 dashes aromatic bitters

GARNISH

1 to 2 tablespoons corn syrup

3 or 4 drops red food coloring

1 mini clothespin

1 mini snack cone

3 to 4 kernels popped popcorn

1. In a small shallow bowl, mix the corn syrup and red food coloring until well combined.

2. Generously rim the glass (see Rimming Guide, page 15) with the red corn syrup, letting the excess drip down the sides of the glass. Put the glass aside to allow the syrup to set.

3. In a cocktail shaker filled with ice, add the whiskey, almond liqueur, cherry juice, lemon juice, Goo Goo Muck, and bitters.

4. Shake for 10 to 15 seconds until well chilled.

5. Strain into the serving glass.

6. Pin the snack cone to the side of the glass and fill it with popcorn. If you'd like, add a small piece of dry ice (page 16) or an ice sphere to the drink and serve!

EBONY AND IVORY

Paul McCartney feat. Stevie Wonder: *Tug of War*

What happens when you get two of the most prolific and acclaimed musicians of the twentieth century? Well, you get Paul McCartney and Stevie Wonder perfectly harmonizing an extended metaphor about piano keys and racial harmony. Not everything is as black-and-white as an '80s pop song might lead you to believe, but our take on the White Russian is just that.

1 ounce heavy cream

½ ounce Irish cream liqueur

1½ ounces black spiced rum

1 ounce coffee liqueur

3 or 4 dashes black walnut bitters

GARNISH

Dutch-processed cocoa powder or dark chocolate shavings

1. In a small bowl, use a milk frother or hand mixer to whip together the heavy cream and Irish cream until thickened but still pourable. Alternatively, pour the heavy cream and Irish cream into a cold cocktail shaker and shake for about 30 seconds until thickened but still pourable.

2. In a rocks glass, combine the black spiced rum, coffee liqueur, and black walnut bitters and stir to combine.

3. Add a large ice cube to the glass.

4. Top with the white chocolate and cream mixture.

5. Garnish with cocoa powder.

GLASS: SOUR OR DELMONICO (NO ICE) OR ROCKS (WITH LARGE ICE)
ICE: STANDARD • **SERVES**: 1

GOODY TWO SHOES

Adam Ant: *Friend or Foe*

You're always going to get one of those goody two shoes coming to your party saying they don't drink. And there's nothing wrong with that! Maybe they're the designated driver and they don't want to get stuck drinking water all night. Whatever the reason, we have just the solution. Besides, who doesn't want to eat edible glitter?!

1 ounce Addicted to Shrub (page 9) or strawberry kombucha

1 ounce lemon juice

1 egg white

1 ounce Milli Vanilli (page 8) or Smooth Operator (page 8)

4 or 5 dashes aromatic bitters

GARNISH
Aromatic bitters
Edible glitter

1. In a cocktail shaker, combine the Addicted to Shrub, lemon juice, egg white, Milli Vanilli, and bitters.

2. Shake for 25 to 35 seconds until foamy.

3. Fill the shaker with ice.

4. Shake for another 10 to 15 seconds until well chilled.

5. Strain into the serving glass. If using a rocks glass, add ice first.

6. Garnish with aromatic bitters and edible glitter.

Tip: To create Adam Ant stripes, use a dropper to carefully place drops of bitters onto the foam in two parallel rows. Then, using a toothpick or skewer, gently draw through the drops to create two lines. Alternatively, for more precise lines, add some bitters to a small spray bottle. Use scissors and a piece of paper to create a double-line stencil and then lay it over the drink. Spray the bitters through the stencil.

FUN FACTS: This song was Adam Ant's answer to the incredulity he would experience when being asked about his sobriety by the press. Although he was one of the most popular performers in the United Kingdom throughout the early '80s, "Goody Two Shoes" was his first and biggest hit in the United States, thanks mainly to MTV, which introduced America to his wild charismatic persona.

GLASS: GLASS MUG • ICE: NONE • SERVES: 1

AFRICA

Toto: *Toto IV*

It doesn't matter where you are in the world, "Africa" will follow you, which is ironic considering it was almost left off Toto's soft-rock banger album due to fears of inauthenticity. As founding band member Steve Lukather said, "'I bless the rains down in Africa . . .' What does that mean? We're a bunch of white guys from North Hollywood." The self-awareness is certainly appreciated. Still, the track was a massive success and helped Toto win six Grammy awards in 1983—and has surely helped you remember what the tallest mountain on the continent is on several a trivia night.

2 rooibos tea bags

1 cup boiling water

3 ounces whole milk or full-fat oat milk

¾ ounce Golden Brown (page 7)

1½ ounces aged rum

1 ounce Amarula® cream liqueur or other cream liqueur

GARNISH

1 dehydrated lemon wheel

FUN FACTS: Despite its wild success, "Africa" was the last song recorded for *Toto IV*. Jeff Porcaro considered saving "Africa" for a solo album, as the other members of the band didn't think it sounded like a Toto song. At the time, the band were more focused on the album's lead single, "Rosanna." Whew!

1. In a small saucepan, brew the tea in the boiling water for 6 to 7 minutes.

2. In the meantime, steam the milk with a milk steamer or frother. Keep in mind that your appliance's minimum amount of milk might be slightly more than what is required for this drink. If you don't have any milk-steaming appliances, pour the milk into a mason jar (with no lid) and microwave for 1 to 2 minutes until hot. Cover with a lid and, using oven mitts, shake the milk for 20 to 30 seconds until frothy.

3. After the tea has steeped, remove the tea bags and stir in the Golden Brown until well combined.

4. Pour the rum and Amarula into the serving glass.

5. Pour in the hot tea, leaving an inch or two for the steamed milk, and stir to combine.

6. Top with steamed milk and garnish with a dehydrated lemon wheel.

TAINTED LOVE

Soft Cell: *Non-Stop Erotic Cabaret*

We were inspired by the song's original video, which is probably as odd as you might expect from a single from an album called *Non-Stop Erotic Cabaret*. Sure, they ended up making a second, ostensibly more "normal" video later, but we prefer to remember the version with piranhas in a fish tank, someone in preppy cricket gear, and vocalist Marc Almond doing a look that could be best described as a mashup of Cleopatra and Julius Caesar. That's the '80s for you. The drink is bittersweet because of the gentian, slightly spicy and floral, with a whole poisoned apple thing going on.

1½ ounces apple brandy

¾ ounce gentian liqueur

½ ounce Goo Goo Muck (page 7)

1 ounce lemon juice

1 or 2 dashes floral bitters

2 or 3 dashes Hurts So Good (page 9) or other spicy bitters

½ ounce dry red wine

GARNISH

Honeycomb or a small pomegranate piece with arils attached

Cocktail skewer

1. In a cocktail shaker filled with ice, add the apple brandy, gentian liqueur, Goo Goo Muck, lemon juice, floral bitters, and Hurts So Good.

2. Shake for 10 to 15 seconds until well chilled.

3. Strain into the serving glass.

4. Add ice until the glass is two-thirds full.

5. Holding a spoon on the surface of the drink, slowly pour the wine onto the spoon, letting overflow onto the drink. The wine should settle on top.

6. Garnish with a skewered piece of honeycomb.

FUN FACTS: This song is a cover, the original being a '60s soul cut composed by Ed Cobb. It was sung by Gloria Jones, who was famously dating Marc Bolan of T. Rex before he died. Jones has said in interviews that she considers the Soft Cell version of "Tainted Love" to be the best one.

SEXUAL HEALING

Marvin Gaye: *Midnight Love*

Baby, now let's make love drinks tonight! Is there a song more apt to get you in the mood than "Sexual Healing"? It's not exactly subtle, but sometimes it's better to just say what you want. Rose petals not included, but feel empowered to let this martini riff inspire you to step up your romance game, even if your love affair is just with yourself.

5 or 6 fresh raspberries

1½ ounces Cognac

½ ounce raspberry liqueur

½ ounce Smooth Operator (page 8)

1 ounce lemon juice

3 or 4 dashes chocolate bitters

2 or 3 dashes rose bitters or
1 or 2 drops rose water

1 egg white or 2 tablespoons
aquafaba

GARNISH
Dried or fresh rose petals and/or
fresh raspberries

1. In a cocktail shaker, muddle the raspberries until mostly crushed (see Muddling Guide, page 14).

2. Add the Cognac, raspberry liqueur, Smooth Operator, lemon juice, chocolate bitters, rose bitters, and egg white.

3. Shake for 30 to 35 seconds.

4. Fill the shaker with standard ice.

5. Shake for another 10 to 15 seconds until well chilled.

6. Double-strain into the serving glass using a fine-mesh strainer. Shake the cocktail shaker to get as much of the foam onto the drink as possible.

7. Garnish with dried rose petals and/or fresh raspberries.

FUN FACTS: Before his solo career, Marvin was a drummer for major Motown acts like The Supremes, Stevie Wonder, The Marvelettes, and more. He also was a member of The Moonglows.

GLASS: HURRICANE • **ICE:** STANDARD • **SERVES:** 1

I WANT A NEW DRUG

Huey Lewis & The News: *Sports*

You want a new drug? Unlike 1983, in most of the USA, you can legally use cannabidiol, also known as CBD, to enhance your beverage. If you're in a more permissive part of the country, you can mix this with a little bit of the devil's lettuce juice. Just make sure you have some eyedrops handy because this could make your eyes red. Sit back, relax, and get ready to go back to the future. Hoverboard not included.

Water-soluble CBD tincture (manufacturer's-recommended single dose)

2 ounces aged rum or nonalcoholic rum alternative

4 ounces pineapple juice

1 ounce orange juice

½ ounce lime juice

1 ounce cream of coconut syrup

2 or 3 drops tropical bitters (optional)

GARNISH

Grated nutmeg

Pineapple slices

Pineapple leaves or mint sprigs

Maraschino cherries

1. In a cocktail shaker filled with ice, add the CBD tincture, rum, pineapple juice, orange juice, lime juice, cream of coconut syrup, and bitters (if using).

2. Shake for 15 to 20 seconds until well chilled and foamy.

3. Strain into a serving glass two-thirds filled with ice.

4. Garnish with grated nutmeg, pineapple slices, pineapple leaves, and maraschino cherries.

FUN FACTS: In 1984, Huey Lewis sued Ray Parker Jr. for stealing the melody from "I Want a New Drug" on his hit "Ghostbusters," the theme song for the eponymous film. In a 2004 article for *Premiere* magazine, the *Ghostbusters* filmmakers admitted to using the song as temporary background music in many scenes. They also stated that they had offered to hire Huey Lewis & The News to write the main theme, but the band had declined. The filmmakers then gave the film footage, with Lewis's song in the background, to Parker to help him write the theme song.

GLASS: STEMLESS WINEGLASS OR HIGHBALL • **ICE**: STANDARD • **SERVES**: 1

I'VE GOT A CRUSH ON YOU

Linda Ronstadt and Nelson Riddle and His Orchestra: *What's New*

How do you even tell someone you like them anymore? Can you just say, "I've got a crush on you," like this Ronstadt cover of a George Gershwin tune? Quote the kids of today: cringe. Are you one of those nervous Nellies who gets anxious and chain-vapes when that special someone is around? Maybe just offer them this delicious drink and pour out your heart.

2 ounces tequila

½ ounce ginger liqueur or ginger juice

1 ruby red grapefruit

½ ounce prickly pear syrup or prickly pear purée

2 to 3 ounces pink grapefruit soda, chilled

GARNISH

Honey or grapefruit juice, for the rim

Black lava salt, for the rim

Dehydrated pink dragon fruit slice, prickly pear candy, or ruby grapefruit slice

1. Rim the glass with honey and black lava salt (see Rimming Guide, page 15).

2. Juice the grapefruit with a hand juicer. You want about 2 to 3 ounces of juice.

3. In a cocktail shaker filled with ice, add the tequila, ginger liqueur, grapefruit juice, and prickly pear syrup.

4. Shake for 10 to 15 seconds until well chilled.

5. Strain into the serving glass and add ice until the glass is two-thirds full.

6. Top with pink grapefruit soda.

7. Garnish with a dehydrated pink dragon fruit slice.

99 Luftballoons

Nena: *Nena*

For those of you that *spreche kein Deutsch*, these ninety-nine balloons are nothing more than red balloons floating in the sky. The English lyrics are entirely different from the original German, in which the balloons being mistaken for a UFO chaotically leads to a nuclear war that leaves just one balloon behind. The '80s were an eclectic time. Not everything came out of New York, Los Angeles, and some dreary town in England. Germans were making hits, too. Shout-out to Alphaville.

3 ounces pineapple juice

¾ ounce gin

¾ ounce sloe gin

½ ounce kirsch

½ ounce lime juice

½ ounce Sweet Dreams (page 6) or other grenadine

¼ ounce orange liqueur

¼ ounce Jägermeister®

2 or 3 dashes aromatic bitters

GARNISH

2 to 4 stemmed maraschino cherries or 1 red lollipop

1. In a cocktail shaker filled with ice, add the pineapple juice, gin, sloe gin, kirsch, lime juice, Sweet Dreams, orange liqueur, Jägermeister, and bitters.

2. Shake vigorously for 15 to 20 seconds until well chilled and foamy.

3. Strain into a serving glass two-thirds filled with standard ice.

4. Garnish with skewered cherries.

Fun Facts: While at a June 1982 concert by The Rolling Stones in West Berlin, Nena's guitarist Carlo Karges noticed that balloons were being released. He thought about what might happen if they floated over the Berlin Wall to the Soviet sector and were mistaken for aircrafts, starting a panic and making the Cold War hot over nothing.

GLASS: DOUBLE ROCKS OR OTHER LOWBALL • **ICE:** STANDARD • **SERVES:** 1

BLUE MONDAY

New Order: *12-inch single*

They were transformed via tragedy from the morose Joy Division into the revolutionary New Order. Now behold: arguably the greatest synth-pop band of all time has inspired a bevvie that will cure anyone with a case of the proverbial Mondays. That's right. All you have to do is queue this song up on your device of choice, wait for the drum machine kick in, and dance the blue wave away. Even the biggest Monday hater, Garfield, might be thinking TGIM after having a hair of this dog.

1½ ounces blueberry rum or vodka

¾ ounce blue curaçao

¾ ounce cream of coconut syrup

1 ounce lime juice

1 ounce coconut milk (from a carton, not a can)

2 or 3 drops When Doves Cry (page 8)

GARNISH

Lime juice, for the rim

Flaky sea salt, for the rim

Dehydrated lime wheel or fresh lime wheel

Melon balls, blueberries, or cocktail cherries

1 cocktail skewer

1. Rim the glass with lime juice and flaky sea salt (see Rimming Guide, page 15).

2. Fill the serving glass with standard ice.

3. In a cocktail shaker filled with ice, add the blueberry rum, blue curaçao, cream of coconut syrup, lime juice, coconut milk, and When Doves Cry.

4. Shake for 10 to 15 seconds until well chilled.

5. Strain into the serving glass.

6. Garnish with a dehydrated lime wheel and skewered melon balls, blueberries, and/or cocktail cherries.

FUN FACTS: **"Blue Monday" is the best-selling twelve-inch single of all time and is considered one of the most influential electronica songs. Synth-pop was already huge in British popular music, but this was arguably the first British dance record to cross over to the New York club scene. The lyrics were written by the group's guitarist and lead singer Bernard Sumner, who (along with the rest of the band) admitted to being under the influence of LSD while writing the song.**

THYME AFTER THYME

Cyndi Lauper: *She's So Unusual*

Get it? It's a play on Cyndi Lauper's "Time After Time." Unlike Time, Cyndi is timeless. She became the first female with four top-five hits on the *Billboard* Hot 100 when her debut album released in 1983 and both *Rolling Stone* and MTV have listed the track "Time After Time" as one of the 100 Greatest Pop Songs of all time. When you look up "'80s icon," Cyndi's picture is next to the definition. If you could "Weird Science" a person from the '80s but in the form of a drink (not as Kelly LeBrock), this is what the Memotech MTX 512 would make.

RHUBARB AND THYME SYRUP

1 cup chopped rhubarb*

1 cup granulated sugar

1 cup water

4 thyme sprigs

DRINK

1 ounce gin

2 ounces Aperol®

1 to 2 ounces tangerine or orange juice

¾ ounce rhubarb and thyme syrup

½ ounce lemon juice

2 to 3 ounces prosecco or club soda

GARNISH

Orange wheels

Thyme sprigs

*If rhubarb is out of season, use fresh strawberries.

1. In a small saucepan, combine the rhubarb, sugar, water, and thyme and bring to a boil over medium high heat. Turn down and let simmer for 15 to 20 minutes, or until the rhubarb breaks down and becomes mushy.

2. Strain first through a colander and then a fine-mesh sieve, removing as much of the solids as possible. Use immediately once cooled or store in the refrigerator for up to 3 weeks.

3. In the serving glass, pour the gin, Aperol, tangerine juice, rhubarb and thyme syrup, and lemon juice and stir to combine.

4. Fill the glass two-thirds full with standard ice, then top with prosecco and/or club soda.

5. Garnish with orange wheels and thyme sprigs and serve!

FUN FACTS: In 1983, Lauper had nearly finished wrapping *She's So Unusual*. However, producer Rick Chertoff wanted one more track, so Cyndi and cowriter Rob Hyman of The Hooters went back to the studio to record the song that became "Time After Time." It was Cyndi's first number one single. The song's title comes from the 1979 science fiction film of the same name.

EVERYTHING COUNTS

Depeche Mode: *Construction Time Again*

It's a synth-pop sensation in a glass. Greed might have been good in the '80s, but Depeche Mode were already positioning themselves in the corner of hip anticapitalists. Yeah, the grabbing hands really do grab all they can. There are aspects of this song that are timeless—how many times have you been taken in by "a suntan and grin"?—but there are others that are more of their time, such as the subtle shots at South Korea's then-dictator Chun Doo-hwan and the countries doing business with him. And folks say that Gen Z is political.

1 Asian pear, cored and roughly chopped (or 3 to 4 ounces pear juice)

½ ounce lemon juice

2½ ounces soju, chilled

½ ounce Pour Some Sugar on Me (page 6) or other simple syrup

2 to 4 dashes pear bitters or ginger bitters (optional)

Pinch gold luster dust (optional)

3 to 4 ounces ginger ale

GARNISH

Gold leaf or gold luster dust

Thinly sliced pear or ginger

1. In a blender, combine the pear and lemon juice. Purée until smooth, adding just enough water to get things moving, as needed.

2. Pass the purée through a fine-mesh strainer directly into the serving glass—you could also use cheesecloth or a nut milk bag. Squeeze or press on the solids to get as much juice out as possible. If using premade pear juice, simply pour it into the serving glass.

3. In the serving glass, pour the soju, Pour Some Sugar on Me, bitters, and luster dust (if using). Stir until well combined.

4. Fill the serving glass two-thirds full with standard ice.

5. Top with ginger ale.

6. Garnish with gold leaf and a pear.

FUN FACTS: *Construction Time Again* was the first album to feature Depeche Mode's classic band lineup, with Alan Wilder replacing Vincent Clarke on keyboards. "This is really the first Depeche Mode album," band member Andy "Fletch" Fletcher told *Vice* magazine.

GLASS: COUPE OR MARGARITA • **ICE:** SPHERE-SHAPED • **SERVES:** 1

THE KILLING MOON

Echo & the Bunnymen: *Ocean Rain*

Though a classic of the *120 Minutes* era of MTV, Echo & the Bunnymen didn't truly get their flowers for this classic track until it turned up in 2001's *Donnie Darko*, where the song's gloomy yet anthemic vibes fit right in with a classic Jake Gyllenhaal performance. Lead singer Ian McCulloch credits God for the lyrics "fate up against your will," so cheers to divine inspiration! The band also reversed the chords from David Bowie's "Space Oddity" for the intro. Sadly, neither the Starman nor the Lord of the Heavens got a songwriting credit.

2 ounces rye whiskey

½ ounce lemon juice

½ ounce Goo Goo Muck (page 7) or other spiced syrup

¼ ounce red bittersweet amaro

4 or 5 dashes aromatic bitters

2 ounces blood orange juice*

GARNISH

Smooth Operator (page 8) or corn syrup, for the rim

Red sanding sugar, for the rim

Salt, for the rim

*If blood oranges or premade blood orange juice aren't available, use cranberry juice instead.

1. Rim the glass with Smooth Operator, red sanding sugar, and salt (see Rimming Guide, page 15).

2. Add an ice sphere to the serving glass.

3. In a cocktail shaker filled with ice, add the rye whiskey, lemon juice, Goo Goo Muck, amaro, bitters, and blood orange juice.

4. Shake for 10 to 15 seconds until well chilled.

5. Strain into the serving glass.

FUN FACTS: **David Bowie's "Space Oddity" was crucial to the song's formation. "I played David Bowie's 'Space Oddity' backwards, then started messing around with the chords," lead singer Ian McCulloch recalled to *The Guardian*. "By the time I'd finished, it sounded nothing like 'Space Oddity.'"**

What's Love Got to Do with It

Tina Turner: *Private Dancer*

Tina Turner is the personification of perseverance and heart. The Queen of Rock 'n' Roll reminded everyone who she was when she dropped *Private Dancer* at the age of forty-five. It ended up as the ninth-best-selling album of the decade—an amazing comeback—and was included in the Library of Congress's National Recording Registry for being "culturally, historically, or aesthetically significant" three years before her 2023 death. 1984 was a great year for albums, between *Purple Rain, Born in the U.S.A., Diamond Life*, etc., but if you turned on MTV or tuned into the radio that year, you wouldn't have had to wait long to catch a track by Tina.

1 ounce Tennessee whiskey or bourbon

¼ ounce Pour Some Sugar on Me (page 6) or other simple syrup

1 ounce sweet (red) vermouth

3 or 4 dashes aromatic bitters

1 or 2 dashes orange bitters

2 to 3 ounces champagne, chilled

GARNISH

Bourbon cherry

Orange peel

1. In a mixing glass filled with ice, add the whiskey, Pour Some Sugar on Me, vermouth, and bitters.

2. Stir in a counterclockwise motion for 20 to 25 seconds until well chilled.

3. Strain into the serving glass.

4. Top with chilled champagne.

5. Garnish with a bourbon cherry and orange peel.

Fun Facts: This song marked Tina Turner's comeback. She initially reached the pop charts in 1960 with her husband Ike, with their biggest hit being a 1971 cover of "Proud Mary." Tina left Ike in 1976, leaving her career in limbo until "What's Love Got to Do with It" brought her back into the spotlight a full thirteen years after "Proud Mary." More hits followed, solidifying her status as a music icon.

GLASS: HIGHBALL, MASON JAR, OR PINT GLASS • **ICE:** STANDARD • **SERVES:** 1

BORN IN THE U.S.A.

Bruce Springsteen: *Born in the U.S.A.*

Bruce Springsteen became a mid-'80s fave of the ultra-patriotic crowd just by slapping an American flag on his album cover and putting U.S.A. in a song title. Take a moment to read the lyric sheet, though, and it isn't hard to tell that Bruce was telling a different story.

1 egg yolk or 2 ounces heavy cream

4 tablespoons sweetened condensed milk

½ teaspoon ground Saigon cinnamon

1½ ounces bourbon

¼ ounce mezcal

½ ounce Golden Brown (page 7)

4 ounces concentrated cold-brew coffee

GARNISH

Star anise

Ground Saigon cinnamon

1. In a small bowl, use a hand mixer to beat together the egg yolk, sweetened condensed milk, and cinnamon for about 2 minutes until it becomes pale and fluffy.

2. In the serving glass, pour the bourbon, mezcal, Golden Brown, and cold-brew coffee. Stir to combine.

3. Add ice until the glass is two-thirds full.

4. Pour or spoon the condensed milk and egg yolk custard into the top of the glass. It should float at the top until stirred.

5. Garnish with star anise and Saigon cinnamon and serve!

PURPLE RAIN

Prince and The Revolution: *Purple Rain*

Believe it or not, when the movie *Purple Rain* was developed, it was seen as a big risk. A musician demanding to act instead of just following up his smash album *1999*? Studios turned it down and tried to replace Prince with someone more recognized for acting but, in the end, talent and the magic of the year 1984 prevailed. Indulge in a cocktail as vibrant and unforgettable as Prince's legendary album. The Purple Rain isn't just a delicious drink, it's a journey through a musical masterpiece that defined a generation. Crank up the music, raise a glass, and let this cocktail transport you to a world of electrifying sound and unforgettable taste.

2 ounces Empress 1908® gin or other indigo gin

1 ounce lemon juice

½ ounce maraschino liqueur

½ ounce parfait amour

1 egg white or 2 tablespoons aquafaba

1 or 2 drops When Doves Cry (page 8)

1 or 2 drops purple food coloring, for extra vibrancy (optional)

GARNISH

1 violet or other edible purple flower or use candied violets

1. In a cocktail shaker, combine the gin, lemon juice, maraschino liqueur, parfait amour, egg white, When Doves Cry, and food coloring (if using).

2. Shake for 30 to 35 seconds until very foamy.

3. Fill the shaker with standard ice.

4. Shake for another 10 to 15 seconds until well chilled.

5. Strain into the serving glass and allow the foam to separate, then garnish with a violet.

FUN FACTS: In a December 2013 interview with *Mojo* magazine, Stevie Nicks revealed that Prince had asked her to collaborate on the title track. "I've still got [the demo cassette] with the whole instrumental track and a little bit of Prince singing, 'Can't get over that feeling,' or something," the Fleetwood Mac singer recalled. "I told him, 'Prince, I've listened to this a hundred times but I wouldn't know where to start. It's a movie, it's epic.'"

CARIBBEAN QUEEN
(NO MORE LOVE ON THE RUN)

Billy Ocean: *Suddenly*

This future number one single was originally released in the UK under another title, "European Queen", but it failed to make a splash. However, once it released in the US under the title, "Caribbean Queen" it shot up to number one. Now you can share the same dream too, with this sweet and refreshing drink. However, if you want to emulate the video with your own puppet-inspired saxophone solo—complete with strobe light—we recommend you finish your cocktail first.

2 ounces white rum

¾ ounce lime juice

½ ounce pineapple or orange liqueur

¾ ounce coconut cream syrup

1 ounce coconut milk (from a carton, not a can)

½ ounce Smooth Operator (page 8)

GARNISH

Honey, for the rim

Salt or sugar, for the rim

Ground cinnamon, for the rim

Lime wheel

1. Rim the glass with honey, salt, and cinnamon (see Rimming Guide, page 15).

2. In a cocktail shaker filled with ice, add white rum, lime juice, pineapple liqueur, coconut cream syrup, coconut milk, and Smooth Operator.

3. Shake for 10 to 15 seconds until well chilled.

4. Strain into the serving glass.

5. Garnish with a lime wheel.

I Feel for You

Chaka Khan: *I Feel for You*

Can you believe in a world in which a cover of a Prince song might be an improvement on the original? "I Feel for You" was a genre-bending masterpiece that featured Stevie Wonder on harmonica and Melle Mel of Grandmaster Flash and the Furious Five on rhymes, creating a funk-infused dance floor phenomenon. Everyone wants to hear those magical words—I feel for you—but we might also see ourselves asking Chaka Khan to rock us. Why not?

1 ounce unflavored or vanilla vodka

½ ounce crème de violette

½ ounce raspberry liqueur

½ ounce Milli Vanilli (page 8) or other vanilla syrup

2 to 3 ounces sparkling rosé

GARNISH

Lemon twist

1 cocktail cherry

1. In a mixing glass filled with ice, add the vodka, crème de violette, raspberry liqueur, and Milli Vanilli.

2. Stir in a counterclockwise motion for 20 to 25 seconds until well chilled.

3. Strain into the serving glass.

4. Top with chilled champagne.

5. Garnish with a lemon twist and cocktail cherry.

DON'T YOU (FORGET ABOUT ME)

Simple Minds: *The Breakfast Club* (Original Motion Picture Soundtrack)

Who are we kidding here? Unlike the various gadgets listening to your everyday conversations, we don't need electronics to invade your privacy. We're in your minds. We know what you're thinking: There are a million deserving '80s hits that didn't make it in this book. Maybe so, but you better believe we're going to make the perfect brunch drink inspired by the epic needle drop when Judd Nelson's character pumps his fist into the air right as the credits roll. Bless you, John Hughes, for making one of the most parodied moments of the '80s and giving us an excuse to get this drunk before noon rolls around.

1½ ounces vodka

½ ounce peated scotch (optional)

1 tablespoon orange marmalade

¼ ounce orange liqueur

¼ ounce Smooth Operator (page 8)

2 or 3 dashes toasted almond or pecan bitters

GARNISH
Orange twist

1. In a cocktail shaker filled with ice, add the vodka, scotch (if using), marmalade, orange liqueur, Smooth Operator, and bitters.

2. Shake for 10 to 15 seconds until well chilled.

3. Strain into the serving glass.

4. Garnish with an orange twist.

FUN FACTS: Keith Forsey, who wrote the title track for *Flashdance*, and Steve Schiff, a former guitarist in Nina Hagen's band, wrote this song specifically for *The Breakfast Club*. They originally wanted Roxy Music to record it, but they turned down the job. Simple Minds almost did as well, because they wanted to use their own song, "Alive & Kicking," in the film and didn't understand that "Don't You (Forget About Me)" had been written specifically for the film and was the only option. Luckily for everyone, they came around.

CENTERFIELD

John Fogerty: *Centerfield*

This drink is inspired by the most nostalgic of American snack foods: Cracker Jack. Remember when you would pop open a rectangular wax-sealed box that had a novelty prize in it? There would be temporary tattoos, decoder rings, and booklets. Simpler times, those were the days. Speaking of Cracker Jacks, it's the seventh-inning stretch! Ingest enough of these buttery whiskey, rum libations and you'll find yourself shouting: PUT ME IN, COACH! I'M READY TO PLAY!

2 ounces gold rum

½ ounce peanut butter whiskey or hazelnut liqueur

1 ounce butterscotch schnapps

½ ounce Golden Brown (page 7)

1 to 2 ounces milk or half-and-half

GARNISH

Caramel sauce, for the rim

Cracker Jack or caramel corn

Cocktail skewer

1. Rim the serving glass in caramel sauce (see Rimming Guide, page 15).

2. In a cocktail shaker filled with ice, add the gold rum, peanut butter whiskey, butterscotch schnapps, Golden Brown, and milk.

3. Shake for 10 to 15 seconds until well chilled.

4. Strain into the serving glass. Add a large ice cube,
if desired.

5. Garnish with skewered Cracker Jack.

Take On Me

a-ha: *Hunting High and Low*

The music video for a-ha's "Take on Me" was a bit of mid-'80s representation for women who read comics, even if the books don't typically come alive. But if a black-and-white hand tries to pull you into the drink, you better think twice before jumping in. Don't come crying to us when those motorcycle racers try to pummel you. We warned you—one of them has got a wrench, and he's ready to use it!

¾ ounce vodka or white rum

¾ ounce aquavit*

½ ounce triple sec

1 ounce lime juice

¾ ounce orgeat

1 egg white or 2 tablespoons aquafaba

½ ounce black rum, to float (optional)

GARNISH

Luxardo cherry or other black cocktail cherry

Cocktail skewer

*Aquavit is a Scandinavian spirit with either an assertive dill or caraway (licorice-like) flavor, depending on the brand. If you don't like those flavors, swap it with additional vodka or white rum.

1. In a cocktail shaker filled with ice, add the vodka, aquavit, triple sec, lime juice, orgeat, and egg white.

2. Shake for 30 to 35 seconds until well chilled and foamy.

3. Strain into the serving glass.

4. Hold a spoon against the inner sides of the glass. Slowly pour the black rum onto the spoon. It should settle under the foam and above the rest of the drink.

5. Garnish with a skewered cocktail cherry.

Fun Facts: This song became a hit in the United States not in small part because of its innovative music video, in which a comic book character beckons the reader to join him inside the comic. It was created by Michael Patterson and his wife Candace Reckinger, who would later work on other iconic '80s videos like "Opposites Attract" by Paula Abdul, "Impulsive" by Wilson Phillips, and "Luka" by Suzanne Vega.

GLASS: COUPE AND A CORDIAL GLASS • **ICE:** STANDARD • **SERVES:** 1

PART-TIME LOVER

Stevie Wonder: *In Square Circle*

In the '80s, there were all kinds of lovers! Easy lovers. Pretend lovers. The Canadian band Loverboy working for the weekend. Here we salute the best of them all: the part-time lover. If you fall in this category, love is just your side hustle to keep the love lights on. Don't forget why you got in this mess to begin with. It's for the love of the game, my friend.

1½ ounces brandy

1 ounce passion fruit liqueur

1 ounce passion fruit purée

½ ounce Milli Vanilli (page 8) or other vanilla syrup

½ ounce lime juice

2 to 3 ounces sparkling wine, chilled

GARNISH

½ passionfruit or 1 whole passion fruit slice

1. In a cocktail shaker filled with ice, add the brandy, passion fruit liqueur, passion fruit purée, Milli Vanilli, and lime juice.

2. Shake for 10 to 15 seconds until well chilled.

3. Strain into the serving glass.

4. Garnish with passion fruit.

5. In a separate smaller glass, pour the sparkling wine.

6. Use the sparkling wine as a palate cleanser in between sips.

RUNNING UP THAT HILL

Kate Bush: *Hounds of Love*

Sure, everyone says they're a Kate Bush fan now, but where were you when Kate was swinging a sword and singing about Emily Brontë books? We're here to say it's OK to admit it if you found out about this one-woman synth jam from *Stranger Things*. Kate Bush isn't likely to complain about your come-lately fandom: having written and produced the song herself, she owns 100 percent of the publishing and reportedly made $2.3 million in streaming royalties in one month off the thirty-four-year-old song. Every '80s act is sending their Spotify link to the producers at Netflix, hoping for lightning to strike twice.

4 or 5 dried butterfly pea flowers

¾ cup water

2 ounces gin

½ ounce peach schnapps

½ ounce falernum

1½ ounces grapefruit juice

3 or 4 dashes peach bitters or citrus bitters

GARNISH

Grapefruit or lemon peel, cut into a lightning bolt shape

1. Add the butterfly pea flowers to a cup or mug and cover with the water.

2. Let the tea steep for 2 hours, then strain out the flowers. Alternatively, brew the tea in boiling hot water for 5 to 6 minutes, then strain out the flowers and let the tea cool to room temperature.

3. To a cocktail shaker filled with ice, add the gin, peach schnapps, falernum, grapefruit juice, and bitters.

4. Shake for 10 to 15 seconds until well chilled.

5. Strain into the serving glass.

6. Add ice until the glass is two-thirds full.

7. Slowly pour in the brewed butterfly tea to fill.

8. Garnish with a citrus peel lightning bolt, if desired. Stir before drinking.

FUN FACTS: Kate Bush not only wrote her own songs but, beginning with her 1982 album *The Dreaming*, also took on the role of producer—a rare achievement, particularly for a female artist at the time. Prior to Bush, the only woman who both wrote and produced her own music at this level was Joni Mitchell.

How Will I Know

Whitney Houston: *Whitney Houston*

"How Will I Know" is a perfect time capsule of the decade. We were shyer back then, and we didn't have the luxury of texting someone and had to betray our feelings by actually making a phone call. You were too shy! Can't speak! If you wanted to know what someone was doing, you had to call their landline and have that awkward conversation with a parent wondering if they'd see you in church that Sunday. Their sibling might pick up the other line, creating extra drama. Let's all just appreciate the current era of personal cell phones that let us avoid as much awkward human interaction as possible.

½ ounce prickly pear syrup or Sweet Dreams (page 6)

1 ounce passion fruit purée

2½ ounces white rum

2 teaspoons blueberry syrup or blueberry jam

2 ounces coconut milk (from a carton, not a can)

GARNISH

Sliced white dragon fruit

1. In the serving glass, pour the prickly pear syrup and passion fruit purée and use a spoon to mix a little.

2. Add ice to the serving glass until it is two-thirds full.

3. In a cocktail shaker, combine the rum, blackberry syrup, and coconut milk.

4. Shake for 10 to 15 seconds until well chilled.

5. Strain into the serving glass.

6. Garnish with a white dragon fruit slice.

FUN FACTS: This song was originally written by George Merrill and Shannon Rubicam to be performed by Janet Jackson, but Janet's team passed on the song because it wasn't the right time. She was in the middle of making her *Control* album.

CONTROL

Janet Jackson: *Control*

Unleash your inner icon with a cocktail that embodies the fierce independence of Janet Jackson's career-defining hit, "Control." This anthem isn't for the faint of heart, and neither is our juice. Breaking out from the shadow of her famous brother (you might have heard of him, Mike or something), Janet made a statement with this track. This drink makes a statement as well. It's for those who refuse to be boxed in and demand to be heard. So raise a glass, savor the power, and let your inner control freak shine.

2 ounces black vodka*

½ ounce lemon juice

½ ounce Milli Vanilli (page 8) or other vanilla syrup

¾ ounce maraschino liqueur

1 ounce black cherry juice

2 or 3 dashes cherry bitters

GARNISH

Lemon twist

Maraschino cherry

Blue cherry or blueberry (optional)

*If you can't find black vodka, add black food coloring or ½ teaspoon of activated charcoal to the shaker.

1. In a cocktail shaker filled with ice, add the black vodka, lemon juice, Milli Vanilli, maraschino liqueur, black cherry juice, and bitters.

2. Shake for 10 to 15 seconds until well chilled.

3. Strain into the serving glass.

4. Garnish with a lemon twist, maraschino cherry, and blue cherry (if using).

FUN FACTS: "*Control* came from the heart," Janet once told the *Los Angeles Times*. "It was all about stepping out, taking control of your life . . . a certain point in your life when you ask yourself who you are and what you want to do." *Control* was Janet's third album, but the first after severing her business with her father and former manager, Joseph Walter Jackson. It became her first album to top the *Billboard* 200 albums chart.

DANGER ZONE

Kenny Loggins: *Top Gun* (Original Motion Picture Soundtrack)

We try not to endorse any particular brands, but you don't want to be in the sky without your wingman (Grey) Goose on this one. It's called the Danger Zone for a reason: This shot is hot. A full-throttle experience of daring maneuvers and pumping adrenaline. Like the shirtless beach volleyball scene in the film. Wait, what were we talking about again?

2 or 3 slices of ghost chile pepper (or hot pepper of your choice)

2 ounces bourbon or rye whiskey

1 ounce ancho chile liqueur

1 ounce lime juice

4 ounces tomato juice or Bloody Mary mix

½ ounce Worcestershire sauce

½ teaspoon prepared horseradish

2 or 3 dashes hot sauce

¼ teaspoon garlic or celery salt

2 or 3 dashes Hurts So Good (page 9) or other spicy bitters (optional)

GARNISH

Hot honey, for the rim

Chipotle seasoning or chile-lime seasoning, for the rim

Candied bacon or maple bacon

Hot pickled vegetables or olives

Whole pickled chile peppers

1. Rim the glass with hot honey and chipotle seasoning (see Rimming Guide, page 15).

2. In the serving glass, muddle the chile peppers (see Muddling Guide, page 14).

3. Fill the glass halfway with ice and add the bourbon, ancho chile liqueur, lime juice, tomato juice, Worcestershire sauce, horseradish, hot sauce (to taste), garlic (to taste), and Hurts So Good (if using).

4. Stir until well combined.

5. Garnish with candied bacon, hot pickled veggies, and chile peppers.

FUN FACTS: Loggins was a prominent figure in '80s movie soundtracks and had a number-one hit two years earlier with the theme song for the movie *Footloose*.

SLEDGEHAMMER

Peter Gabriel: *So*

Fun fact: The animation studio that produced the great claymation series *Wallace and Gromit* was behind the making of this music video, and Peter Gabriel had to lay under a plate of glass for sixteen hours to make the magic happen. Fortunately, it will take you considerably less time to make this drink. For good reason, this was the most-played music video in MTV history. Remember when they used to play music videos and Kurt Loder was there to snidely report the news? But then again, the '80s didn't have *Ridiculousness*. It's all a give-and-take.

1½ ounces overproof rum

1½ ounces spiced rum

1 ounce banana liqueur

½ ounce Smooth Operator (page 8)

1 ounce lime juice

2 to 3 ounces pineapple juice

2 or 3 dashes aromatic bitters

3 or 4 dashes allspice or pimento bitters (optional)

GARNISH

Rainbow twist lollipop(s) and cotton candy

Pineapple leaves

Citrus slices

Edible flowers

1. In a cocktail shaker filled with standard ice, add the overproof rum, spiced rum, banana liqueur, Smooth Operator, lime juice, pineapple juice, aromatic bitters, and allspice bitters.

2. Shake for 10 to 15 seconds until well chilled.

3. Strain into the serving glass.

4. Add ice to fill.

5. Garnish with rainbow twist lollipops, pineapple leaves, citrus slices, and various edible flowers. In this case, more is more!

6. Note: Go completely over the top with the garnishes! Anything seen in the video will work, except maybe that dancing chicken.

PAPA DON'T PEACH

Madonna: *True Blue*

Madonna is one of those rare artists who can get away with a one-word name like Cleopatra, Cher, Prince, and Beyoncé. But there is and will only ever be one Madonna. If you could break the original bad girl of the '80s into liquid form, it would look and taste something like this. Still probably shouldn't tell your dad, though.

2 ounces bourbon or rye whiskey

1 ounce peach nectar

¾ ounce peach liqueur

3 or 4 dashes peach or orange bitters

3 or 4 ounces prosecco or ginger ale

GARNISH

Peach slices

Mint sprigs

1. In a cocktail shaker filled with ice, add the bourbon, peach nectar, peach liqueur, and bitters.

2. Shake for 10 to 15 seconds until well chilled.

3. Strain into the serving glass.

4. Fill the glass with ice until it is two-thirds full.

5. Top with the prosecco.

6. Garnish with peach slices and mint sprigs.

FUN FACTS: Brian Elliot, the song's writer, said of the song to the *Los Angeles Times:* "I saw it as a sensitive plea for compassion and understanding about a young girl who found herself at a crossroads in life and didn't know where to turn." He added, "Any time a song can galvanize the public and create this kind of debate, it's as much as any pop song can ever hope to be."

CITIES IN DUST

Siouxsie and the Banshees: *Tinderbox*

Easier than unearthing a forgotten civilization, this intoxicant is inspired by Siouxsie and the Banshees and their dance floor classic. Take yourself on a journey to the heart of a lost world while your palate and your eardrums are engulfed! Just like Vesuvius, you'll experience your own eruption of sorts while feeling the power of mother nature (or alcohol, either one).

½ lime

2 ounces black spiced rum

¼ ounce mezcal

½ ounce amaro

½ ounce Goo Goo Muck (page 7)

2 to 3 ounces pomegranate juice

GARNISH

Corn syrup or honey, for the rim

Black lava salt, for the rim

½ lime, juiced

½ ounce overproof rum

1. Rim the serving glass with corn syrup and black lava salt (see Rimming Guide, page 15). Set aside.

2. Squeeze the lime half into a cocktail shaker filled with ice, getting as much juice as you can. Set the lime half aside (do not discard, as we will use it later to garnish).

3. Add the rum, mezcal, amaro, Goo Goo Muck, and pomegranate juice.

4. Shake for 10 to 15 seconds until well chilled.

5. Strain into the serving glass.

6. Fill the serving glass to the top with standard ice.

7. Place the squeezed lime on top of the drink and fill it with the overproof rum. Use a long-necked lighter to light it on fire. Once the fire burns out, you can squeeze any remaining liquid from the charred lime into the drink.

FUN FACTS: This song narrates the fate of Pompeii, the city buried during Mount Vesuvius's eruption in 79 AD. Siouxsie Sioux once told *Creem* magazine that she was inspired by a trip to the region.

MANIC MONDAY

The Bangles: *Different Light*

Honestly, there's nothing uglier than a Manic Monday. The Bangles knew what was up. Have enough of these spritzers and you'll find yourself transported to Sunday, kissing Valentino without a care in the world. Valentino will even make your bed if you're lucky.

½ cup cherries, pitted and halved*

1 ounce vodka

1½ ounces amaretto

1 ounce lime juice

¼ ounce pure maple syrup

1 or 2 drops When Doves Cry (page 8)

2 to 3 ounces club soda

GARNISH

Fresh or bourbon-soaked cherries

*We recommend using either fresh cherries, bourbon-soaked cherries, or a mix of both.

1. In a cocktail shaker, muddle the cherries (see Muddling Guide, page 14).

2. Add the vodka, amaretto, lime juice, maple syrup, and When Doves Cry.

3. Fill the shaker with standard ice.

4. Shake for 10 to 15 seconds until well chilled.

5. Strain into the serving glass.

6. Fill the serving glass two-thirds full with standard ice.

7. Top with club soda to fill.

8. Garnish with fresh cherries.

FUN FACTS: The song was written by Prince under the pseudonym "Christopher," a reference to his character from *Under the Cherry Moon*. The song was originally intended for the group Apollonia 6 but it was removed from their self-titled debut album prior to release. Later, it was offered up to The Bangles by Prince himself, who had taken a liking to the band, particularly Susanna Hoffs. The Bangles recorded the song and made it their own, and the rest is history.

I STILL HAVEN'T FOUND WHAT I'M LOOKING FOR

U2: *Joshua Tree*

From Dublin to the Mojave Desert, U2 still haven't found what they were looking for. It's almost as if they were rattling off all the necessary ingredients for the perfect U2-inspired cocktail. Honey lips. Burning desire. Irish whiskey. All right, that last one is because they're Irish. But Irish people love to represent. Here's a little taste of home for the Dublin boys.

½ ounce crème de cassis or blackberry brandy

1½ ounces Irish whiskey

¾ ounce lime juice

½ ounce Smooth Operator (page 8)

3 or 4 drops Hurts So Good (page 9) (optional)

3 ounces orange juice

GARNISH

Lime juice, for the rim

Mesquite powder or smoked salt, for the rim

Turbinado sugar, for the rim

Dehydrated citrus wheel

Cocktail cherries

Cocktail skewer

1. Rim the serving glass with lime juice, mesquite powder, and sugar (see Rimming Guide, page 15).

2. Pour the crème de cassis into the serving glass.

3. Add standard ice to the serving glass until it is two-thirds full.

4. In a cocktail shaker filled with standard ice, add the Irish whiskey, lime juice, Smooth Operator, Hurts So Good (if using), and orange juice.

5. Shake vigorously for 15 to 20 seconds until well chilled and lightly foamy.

6. Strain into the serving glass.

7. Garnish with a dehydrated citrus wheel and skewered cocktail cherries.

FUN FACTS: The working title for this song was "Under the Weather." This song, and many of the songs on *Joshua Tree*, were inspired by gospel music. Bono has described the song as "a kind of gospel song with a restless spirit."

ALONE

Heart: *Bad Animals*

This slushie will chill you to the bone. Just like the chills that run down your spine when you hear Heart's Ann and Nancy Wilson harmonize with perfect precision. You can power a small city with the dynamics of this song, so the drink needed to have some electricity, too. This serves up two or three margarita glasses, so call your sisters from another mister and have a heart-to-heart.

4 ounces sloe gin

375 milliliters rosé wine

1 cup frozen strawberries

1 ounce Sweet Dreams (page 6) or other grenadine

5 or 6 dashes aromatic bitters

2 cups ice

GARNISH

Fresh strawberries

Mint sprigs

1. In a blender, combine the sloe gin, rosé, strawberries, Sweet Dreams, bitters, and ice.

2. Blend for 1 to 2 minutes on high speed until smooth.

3. Pour into the serving glass.

4. Garnish with strawberries and mint sprigs.

FUN FACTS: In 1991, the Wilson sisters became co-owners of a Seattle recording studio, named Bad Animals after this album. The studio hosted recordings by Soundgarden, REM, Nirvana, Neil Young, Johnny Cash, and Pearl Jam.

Also, this song is actually a cover of an i-Ten song.

LA BAMBA

Los Lobos: *La Bamba* (Original Motion Picture Soundtrack)

Covers are magical things. When Manfred Mann's Earth Band covered "Blinded by the Light," it wasn't Bruce Springsteen's anymore. It's unfortunate we didn't get all that much music from Ritchie Valens, but East L.A. legends Los Lobos did bust out to a new level of fame with their version of Valens's most memorable song. A great cover reinterprets a memory, and you'll take your own journey experiencing this riff on a tres leches cake but in a boozy glass.

¼ cup aguardiente de caña, cachaça, rum, or tequila

¼ cup peanut butter or dulce de leche sauce

½ cup evaporated milk

1 ounce horchata liqueur

1 ounce sweetened condensed milk

½ teaspoon vanilla extract

1 to 2 cups ice

GARNISH

Ground cinnamon

Cinnamon sticks

1. In a blender, combine the aguardiente de caña, peanut butter, evaporated milk, horchata liqueur, sweetened condensed milk, vanilla, and ice (to taste).

2. Blend on high speed for a minute or two, until smooth.

3. Pour into the serving glasses.

4. Garnish with ground cinnamon and cinnamon sticks.

FUN FACTS: Originally a modest hit for Ritchie Valens in 1959, "La Bamba" is a traditional Mexican folk song commonly played at weddings and celebrations. When Los Lobos recorded it for the 1987 biopic about Valens, their rendition became a massive hit, introducing the song to a new generation.

NEVER GONNA GIVE BREW UP

Rick Astley: *Whenever You Need Somebody*

Is this a cocktail or a beer with some spilled spirits? This song prompted
one of the earliest internet pranks, so it stands to reason that its drink deserves
some mischievousness as well. This drink is a subversion of expectations,
like Astley himself, who many were surprised to find out was a redheaded Brit.
We could all use an extra bit of surprise in our life, right?

1½ ounces gin

¾ ounce bittersweet amaro

2 or 3 dashes orange bitters

2 ounces ginger beer

2 to 3 ounces red lager

GARNISH

Orange twist

1. In a serving glass, pour the gin, amaro, and bitters and give it a quick stir.

2. Fill the serving glass two-thirds full with ice.

3. Add the ginger beer, then the lager to fill.

4. Garnish with an orange twist and serve!

HEAVEN IS A PLACE ON EARTH

Belinda Carlisle: *Heaven On Earth*

By 1987, if you lived through the bulk of the '80s, you were probably hoping for some joy and escape. The stock market was crashing, but Belinda Carlisle, lead singer of The Go-Go's, was dancing and bubbling with optimism. It's a good reminder that sometimes, when things are tough, you need to make your own heaven on earth. Sometimes that can be a drink shared with a friend.

6 or 7 fresh or thawed blackberries

1½ ounces vanilla vodka

½ ounce blackberry or raspberry liqueur

½ ounce blueberry syrup

½ ounce lime juice

2 or 3 dashes aromatic bitters

2 to 3 ounces sparkling mineral water

GARNISH

Edible pink flower

Mint sprigs

Fresh blackberries

1. In the serving glass, muddle the blackberries (see Muddling Guide, page 14).

2. Add the vodka, blackberry liqueur, blueberry syrup, lime juice, and bitters.

3. Fill the glass two-thirds full with crushed ice.

4. Swizzle the drink with a swizzle stick or barspoon (or, as a last resort, a straw). You do this by immersing the stick into the glass and holding the shaft in between both palms, quickly moving your hands back and forth, causing the stick to spin rapidly. Do this for about a minute until the glass becomes frosty.

5. Top with sparkling mineral water and more crushed ice.

6. Garnish with an edible pink flower, mint sprigs, and additional blackberries.

FUN FACTS: The video was directed by Diane Keaton.

FAITH

George Michael: *Faith*

Do you remember why Darth Vader force-choked that guy in *Star Wars IV*? He found his lack of faith disturbing. That's right. Even Darth knew that you've got to have faith. Maybe George Michael was talking about a different kind of faith, or maybe he and Vader were on the same cosmic wavelength. Pick up that heart, dust it off, and concoct yourself an adult lemonade.

2 ounces blue raspberry vodka

¾ ounce blue curaçao

¾ ounce lemon juice

¼ ounce Pour Some Sugar on Me (page 6) or other simple syrup

2 or 3 drops When Doves Cry (page 8) or other saline

3 to 4 ounces lemon-lime soda or club soda

GARNISH

Luxardo cherries or other cocktail cherries

Lemon wheels

1. In a cocktail shaker filled with ice, add the vodka, blue curaçao, lemon juice, Pour Some Sugar on Me, and When Doves Cry.

2. Shake for 10 to 15 seconds until well chilled.

3. Strain into the serving glass.

4. Add ice until the glass is two-thirds full.

5. Top with the soda to fill.

6. Garnish with Luxardo cherries and lemon wheels.

FAST CAR

Tracy Chapman: *Tracy Chapman*

Making something from zero is the name of the game. Few '80s musicians know it better than Tracy Chapman. Her self-titled debut album was the second-best-selling record of 1988, breaking through the hair-metal craze and outselling the likes of Bon Jovi, New Kids on the Block, and Metallica. Tracy became the first Black person to win Song of the Year at the 2023 Country Music Awards. We dedicate this to the Tracy Chapmans of the world. Get in that fast car and take us where we have never dared to go. Responsibly, of course.

1 ounce orange juice

½ ounce Addicted to Shrub (page 9)

½ ounce Sweet Dreams (page 6) or other grenadine

4 or 5 dashes Angostura® bitters

2 ounces lemon-lime soda

2 ounces sparkling citrus juice

GARNISH

Sliced cucumber

Lime wheels

Orange wheels

1. In the serving glass, gently muddle the sliced cucumber and citrus wheels (see Muddling Guide, page 14).

2. In a cocktail shaker filled with standard ice, add the orange juice, Addicted to Shrub, Sweet Dreams, and bitters.

3. Shake for 10 to 15 seconds until well chilled.

4. Strain into the serving glass.

5. Add ice until the glass is two-thirds full.

6. Top with lemon-lime soda and sparkling citrus juice.

7. Give it a quick stir.

8. Garnish with a sliced cucumber and citrus wheels.

THE TEA LEAF PROPHECY

Joni Mitchell: *Chalk Mark in a Rain Storm*

We wanted to do something a little different in a world where coffee is the de facto drink for breakfast and happy hour. Joni Mitchell is the definition of cool and classy. Her enticing sound from *Chalk Mark in a Rain Storm* is a mood. The minutia makes this song and drink not for the average Joe who prefers an average cup of joe. For example: don't skip on the orgeat. It's pronounced or-ZHA.

1 tablespoon loose-leaf sencha tea

6 to 8 mint leaves

2½ ounces shōchū or 2 ounces white rum

¾ ounces lime juice

¾ ounce orgeat

2 to 3 ounces club soda

GARNISH

Mint leaves

1. Brew the sencha tea according to the package directions and let the tea cool to room temperature.

2. In the serving glass, muddle the mint until slightly bruised and fragrant (see Muddling Guide, page 14).

3. Add the shōchū, lime juice, orgeat, and 2 ounces of the green tea. Give the drink a stir.

4. Fill the glass two-thirds full with standard ice.

5. Add 2 ounces of the brewed green tea.

6. Top with soda water to fill.

7. Garnish with mint leaves.

Where Is My Mind?

Pixies: *Surfer Rosa*

The mind is a precious thing. It's like a fishbowl of swirling thoughts, urges, and desires. The Swedish Fish are safe to eat. We repeat. Eat the fish. Any drinker worth their weight would tell you to pass on the liquor with the dead worm or scorpion in the bottle. That's just a cheap marketing ploy to take your hard-earned money, which is the complete opposite of what the Pixies are all about. Sure, *Fight Club* got jocks listening, but you and I both know you were there, front row in 1988 at CBGB & OMFUG. How did we know? We gave you a ride. Remember?

2 ounces gin or rhum agricole

¾ ounce sweetened condensed milk or cream of coconut syrup

½ ounce blue curaçao

2 to 3 ounces coconut water

2 or 3 dashes Caribbean bitters or orange bitters

GARNISH

Swedish Fish candies

Grated nutmeg

1. In a cocktail shaker filled with ice, add the gin, sweetened condensed milk, blue curaçao, coconut water, and bitters.

2. Shake for 10 to 15 seconds until well chilled.

3. Strain into a serving glass filled two-thirds full with standard ice.

4. Garnish with Swedish Fish candies and grated nutmeg.

Fun Facts: The group arrived at its name after Joey Santiago selected the word "pixies" from a dictionary, liking its definition of "mischievous little elves."

I'M GONNA BE (500 MILES)

The Proclaimers: *Sunshine on Leith*

500 miles is a long way. But why 500 miles? It's a good number, that's why. If someone told you they were going to walk 50 miles, it would feel wrong and perverted. 5,000 miles would sound stalkerish and creepy. 500 miles is sufficient to prove you're the one they want to wake up next to at the end of the day. Besides, this sweet and strong is a perfect drink to have for a pre- or post-500 mile walk. The whiskey will keep you loose, honey provides essential carbs, while the egg white protein gives a boost for good measure. You're practically shaking a meal. You're welcome.

1½ ounces scotch

1 ounce Drambuie® or honey liqueur

1 ounce lemon juice

2 to 5 drops black walnut bitters

1 egg white

½ ounce half-and-half (optional)

2 to 3 ounces ginger ale

1 egg white or 2 tablespoons aquafaba

GARNISH

Lemon twist

1. In a cocktail shaker, add the scotch, Drambuie, lemon juice, bitters, and egg white.

2. Shake for 50 to 60 seconds until very foamy.

3. Add ice and shake for another 10 to 15 seconds until well chilled.

4. In the serving glass, pour the half-and-half (if using).

5. Strain the contents of the shaker into the serving glass.

6. Add ginger ale to fill.

7. Garnish with a lemon twist.

Fun Facts: The Proclaimers, a brotherly duo, were originally a punk band but were inspired to change their sound after seeing a live performance by Dexys Midnight Runners, known for their hit "Come On Eileen." The frontman of Dexys Midnight Runners, Kevin Rowland, helped them to record their first demo. Most of us in the United States associate this song with the '90s because it wasn't released in North America until the movie *Benny & Joon* came out in 1993, where it was used as the main theme of the film.

STRAIGHT OUTTA COMPTON

N.W.A.: *Straight Outta Compton*

This refreshment is legit straight out of Compton. The only thing missing from the ingredients list are Drake's tears, but we'll settle for our homemade When Doves Cry (page 8). But Compton wasn't always the urban epicenter of American racial discourse: Once upon a time, it was rural land where Black families farmed and raised their families (and cattle, too!). You can still find the Compton Vaqueros trotting around the Richland Farm that was originally established in 1889.

2 ounces tequila

1 ounce lime juice

¾ ounce orange liqueur

¾ ounce agave nectar

2 or 3 drops When Doves Cry (page 8)

3 to 4 ounces malt liquor, chilled

GARNISH

Lime juice, for the rim

Salt, for the rim

Lime wedges

1. Rim the glass with lime juice and sea salt (see Rimming Guide, page 15).

2. In the serving glass, combine the tequila, lime juice, orange liqueur, agave, and When Doves Cry.

3. Give it a quick stir.

4. Add ice until the glass is two-thirds full.

5. Top with malt liquor to fill.

6. Garnish with lime wedges.

FUN FACTS: *Straight Outta Compton* was among the first albums to carry a Parental Advisory sticker. This came just a few years after Tipper Gore was outraged upon hearing the sexually explicit lyrics of Prince's "Darling Nikki" emanating from her young daughter's bedroom.

Posse on Broadway

Sir Mix-a-Lot: *Swass*

Everyone in the '80s was under the impression that hip-hop only came out of Brooklyn or Los Angeles, so who would've thought that the Pacific Northwest would give us Anthony "Sir Mix-a-Lot" Ray? The world was never the same after he whipped out all twelve inches of "Posse on Broadway." There was no putting that genie back in the bottle. But since you've got the genie, you've got three wishes. What was that? You want to drink the best boozy milkshake ever? You don't want to end world hunger? OK. Your wish is our command! POSSE UP!

2 ounces Cognac or brandy

2 ounces vanilla liqueur, strawberry liqueur, or crème de cacao

2 large scoops vanilla, strawberry, or chocolate ice cream

½ cup whole milk

2 tablespoons malted milk powder or powdered milk (optional)

GARNISH

Whipped cream

Cherry

1. In a blender, combine the Cognac, vanilla liqueur, ice cream, whole milk, and malted milk powder.

2. Blend for 1 to 2 minutes until smooth.

3. Pour into the serving glass.

4. Garnish with whipped cream and a cherry.

Fun Facts: The track's deep bass drum sounds were produced using Roland's TR-808 drum machine, mentioned in the lyrics as the "808 kick-drum." Capturing the elongated decay on the twenty-four-inch tape of the time was challenging, but Terry Date, a renowned Seattle recording engineer known for his work with grunge bands, successfully achieved the effect.

GLASS: 3 SHOT GLASSES • ICE: NONE • SERVES: 1

ME MYSELF AND I

De La Soul: *3 Feet High and Rising*

How do you go out of your way to fully embody De La Soul's spirit and impact on culture, music, and the zeitgeist? Trick question: you can't. An easier question is why three layers for this drink? What's the magic number? Well, everything good is in threes. Comedy is in threes; Topic, premise, punchline. The Three Musketeers. Destiny's Child. And so does De La Soul: Maseo, Posdnuos, and the late great Trugoy the Dove. This one is for you, Dave.

PLUG 1 (ME)

¾ ounce coconut rum

¼ ounce blue curaçao

½ ounce mango or peach nectar

PLUG 2 (MYSELF)

½ ounce gold rum

¾ ounce mango or banana liqueur

¼ ounce lime juice

PLUG 3 (I)

½ ounce tequila

¾ ounce strawberry pucker

¼ ounce Sweet Dreams (page 6) or other grenadine

GARNISH

Lime juice or honey, for the rims

Black lava salt or black sanding sugar, for the rims

1. Rim three shot glasses with lime juice and black salt (see Rimming Guide, page 15).

2. To make the plug 1: In a cocktail shaker filled with ice, add the coconut rum, blue curaçao, and mango nectar.

3. Shake for 10 to 15 seconds until well chilled.

4. Strain into one of the shot glasses.

5. Dump the ice and rinse the shaker.

6. To make plug 2: In a cocktail shaker filled with ice, add the gold rum, mango liqueur, and lime juice.

7. Shake for 10 to 15 seconds until well chilled.

8. Strain into a shot glass.

9. Dump the ice and rinse the shaker.

10. To make plug 3: In a cocktail shaker filled with ice, add the tequila, strawberry pucker, and Sweet Dreams.

11. Shake for 10 to 15 seconds until well chilled.

12. Strain into a shot glass.

FUN FACTS: The main groove is sampled from Funkadelic's "(Not Just) Knee Deep." Q-Tip and Ali from A Tribe Called Quest make a cameo appearance.

DON'T WANNA LOSE YOU / SI VOY A PERDERTE

Gloria Estefan: *Cuts Both Ways*

Just like rum, very few things from the '80s age better than Gloria Estefan and her music. We can look back on the life and musical gifts Estefan has lived up to this point without wincing. The Cuban American is a gay rights activist, eight-time Grammy Award Winner, and recipient of the Presidential Medal of Freedom. This refreshing daiquiri is dedicated to her and the rhythm she has given us as a human race. Goes down smoothly every time and straight to your shaking hips.

2 ounces rum

½ ounce maraschino liqueur

1 ounce lime juice, freshly squeezed

2 ounces guava nectar

1 to 2 ounces coconut milk (from a carton, not a can)

1 barspoon Sweet Dreams (page 6) or other grenadine

3 or 4 dashes daiquiri or orange bitters

GARNISH

Honey or corn syrup, for the rim

Coconut flakes, for the rim

Edible pink flowers, lime wheels, and pink guava slices

1. Rim the glass with honey or corn syrup and coconut flakes (see Rimming Guide, page 15).

2. In a cocktail shaker filled with standard ice, add the rum, maraschino liqueur, lime juice, guava nectar, coconut milk, Sweet Dreams, and bitters.

3. Shake for 10 to 15 seconds until well chilled.

4. Strain into the serving glass.

5. Garnish with edible pink flowers, lime wheels, and/or guava slices.

FUN FACTS: This was the first single released by Gloria Estefan not under the banner of Miami Sound Machine. It was her first number one single. The Spanish version of the song, "Si Voy a Perderte," reached number one on *Billboard*'s Hot Latin Tracks.

GLASS: COUPE • **ICE:** NONE • **SERVES:** 1

PAUL'S BOUTIQUE

Beastie Boys: *Paul's Boutique*

The age-old question: how do you classify the Beastie Boys? Are they rap or rock? The B Boys and their musical production are a pretty boutique of elements, like this cocktail. Complicatedly mesmerizing and forward thinking. 105 songs were sampled in the album and one track even had 24 individual samples at an era when there was no Garage Band. All analog. You mix in a little Dickens, Johnny Cash, and Jimi Hendrix and you've got an alcoholic preparation that would have Gilles de Gouberville smiling.

2 ounces applejack or calvados

½ ounce vanilla liqueur

½ ounce Sweet Dreams (page 6) or other grenadine

1 ounce lemon juice

1 egg white

GARNISH

Thinly sliced apple

1 cherry

1. In a cocktail shaker, combine the applejack, vanilla liqueur, Sweet Dreams, lemon juice, and egg white.

2. Shake vigorously for 25 to 30 seconds until foamy.

3. Fill the shaker with standard ice.

4. Shake for another 10 to 15 seconds until well chilled.

5. Strain into the serving glass.

6. Garnish with sliced apples and a cherry.

FUN FACTS: The album was created in collaboration with the Dust Brothers, who were known for their innovative sampling techniques. Although the brothers were initially aiming for a more commercially marketable sound for the album, the Beastie Boys wanted them to craft something more daring and distinctive.

SO ALIVE

Love and Rockets: *Love and Rockets*

What was the inspiration behind this one, you ask? Apparently, Daniel Ash drank a bottle of whiskey when he wrote the song. From Ash: "We were in Blackwing Studios in London. I went down to the cellar where the pool tables were, took a bottle of whiskey with me, and about 45 minutes later I came up and had the song. It was a very magical day." Inspiration comes from the darndest places. Maybe the bold whiskey notes and refreshing mint will help inspire you to write a song that someday might be paid homage to in the form of a sophisticated mixed drink. That's when you'll know you've made it, ladies and germs.

1½ ounces rye whiskey

¾ ounce ancho chile liqueur

¾ ounce lime juice

½ ounce Goo Goo Muck (page 7)

2 or 3 dashes aromatic bitters

1 or 2 dashes Hurts So Good (page 9) or other spicy bitters (optional)

2 to 3 ounces ginger beer

GARNISH

Mint sprigs

Chile mango

Ginger slices or candied ginger

1. In the serving glass, pour the whiskey, ancho liqueur, lime juice, Goo Goo Muck, aromatic bitters, and Hurts So Good. Give it a quick stir.

2. Add standard ice until the glass is two-thirds full.

3. Top with ginger beer to fill.

4. Garnish with mint sprigs, chile mango, and ginger slices.

FUN FACTS: The band's name was taken from the comic book series *Love and Rockets* by the Hernandez brothers. The band is comprised of three former members of Bauhaus: Daniel Ash, Kevin Haskins, and David J.

PUMP UP THE JAM

Technotronic: *Pump Up the Jam*

Do you know why it's jam, not jelly? You can't pump up the jelly. But we've got a surprise for you: there's jam *and* jelly in this drink. Now go make somebody's day and shake up this cocktail at the bar and that booty on the dance floor. You only live once. That we know of, anyway.

2½ ounces genever or tequila blanco

1 tablespoon red pepper jelly

1 tablespoon strawberry jam

1 ounce lime juice

5 or 6 dashes orange bitters

GARNISH

Sliced jalapeños and lime wheels

Sliced fresh strawberries

1. In a cocktail shaker filled with ice, add the genever, red pepper jelly, strawberry jam, lime juice, and bitters.

2. Shake for 10 to 15 seconds until well chilled.

3. Strain into the serving glass.

4. Garnish with jalapeño and/or lime wheels and strawberry slices.

FUN FACTS: Initially, Technotronic's vocalist Ya Kid K was "replaced" by Congolese model Felly Kilingi, who appears lip-syncing in the video and was featured on the first album cover. Ya Kid K was eventually recognized with a repackaged album cover that featured her instead of Felly.

JUST A FRIEND

Biz Markie: *The Biz Never Sleeps*

Everyone's been there. The friend zone. There's nothing wrong with it. Some of the best relationships start as friendships. It's best to handle these kinds of situations with class like Biz did in that funny Mozart cosplay. Raise your goblet and turn the other cheek. You'll find someone to match your freak. There's plenty of fish in the sea.

1½ ounces 100-proof vodka

½ ounce apricot brandy

¾ ounce orange liqueur

½ ounce lemon juice

¼ ounce Smooth Operator (page 8)

2 to 3 ounces champagne, chilled

GARNISH

Lemon twist

1. In a cocktail shaker filled with standard ice, add the vodka, apricot brandy, orange liqueur, lemon juice, and Smooth Operator.

2. Shake for 10 to 15 seconds until well chilled.

3. Strain into the serving glass.

4. Add champagne to fill.

5. Garnish with a lemon twist.

Don't Stop Livin' on A Prayer

Journey: "Don't Stop Believin'" + Bon Jovi: "Livin' on A Prayer"

1½ ounces applejack

½ ounce peated scotch

1 ounce cran-apple juice

4 or 5 dashes aromatic bitters

2 to 3 ounces red wine

1 to 3 ounces lemon-lime soda

GARNISH

Rosemary sprig

1. In the serving glass, pour the applejack, scotch, cran-apple juice, bitters, and wine and give it a quick stir.

2. Fill the glass two-thirds full with ice.

3. Top with lemon-lime soda.

4. Garnish with a rosemary sprig, which you can light on fire, if desired.

Smalltown Boy, West End Girls

Bronski Beat: "Smalltown Boy" + Pet Shop Boys: "West End Girls"

1 ounce gin

1 ounce scotch

½ ounce lime cordial

2 or 3 drops When Doves Cry (page 8)

2 to 3 ounces ginger beer, chilled

6 to 8 dashes aromatic bitters

GARNISH

Lime twist or lime wheels

Cocktail cherries

1 cocktail skewer (optional)

1. In the serving glass, pour the gin, scotch, lime cordial, and When Doves Cry and give it a quick stir.

2. Fill the glass two-thirds full with ice.

3. Add ginger beer almost to the top, leaving about a quarter inch of room.

4. Add the aromatic bitters to float.

5. Garnish with a lime twist and cocktail cherries.

MASHUP!

EVERY ROSE YOU TAKE HAS ITS THORN

The Police: "Every Breath You Take" + Poison: "Every Rose Has Its Thorn"

¾ ounce aged rum

¾ ounce bourbon

½ ounce bittersweet amaro

2 ounces pineapple juice

½ ounce lime juice

½ ounce Sweet Dreams (page 6) or other grenadine

4 or 5 dashes rose bitters or ½ teaspoon rose water

2 or 3 drops Hurts So Good (page 9) or spicy bitters (optional)

GARNISH

Honey or corn syrup, for the rim

Turbinado sugar, for the rim

Dried rose petals, crumbled, for the rim

Cocktail cherries

Cocktail skewer

1. Rim the glass with honey, turbinado sugar, and crumbled dried rose petals (see Rimming Guide, page 15).

2. In a cocktail shaker filled with ice, add the rum, bourbon, amaro, pineapple juice, lime juice, Sweet Dreams, rose bitters, and Hurts So Good (if using).

3. Shake for 15 to 20 seconds until well chilled and foamy.

4. Strain into the serving glass.

5. Garnish with skewered cocktail cherries.

MASHUP!

HUMPTY LIKE THE WOLF

Digital Underground: "The Humpty Dance" + Duran Duran: "Hungry Like the Wolf"

¾ ounce aged rum

¾ ounce bourbon

½ ounce bittersweet amaro

2 ounces pineapple juice

½ ounce lime juice

½ ounce Sweet Dreams (page 6)
or other grenadine

4 or 5 dashes rose bitters
or ½ teaspoon rose water

2 or 3 drops Hurts So Good (page
9) or spicy bitters (optional)

GARNISH

Honey or corn syrup, for the rim

Turbinado sugar, for the rim

Dried rose petals, crumbled, for
the rim

Cocktail cherries

Cocktail skewer

1. Rim the glass with honey, turbinado sugar,
and crumbled dried rose petals (see Rimming
Guide, page 15).

2. In a cocktail shaker filled with ice, add the
rum, bourbon, amaro, pineapple juice, lime
juice, Sweet Dreams, rose bitters, and Hurts So
Good (if using).

3. Shake for 15 to 20 seconds until well chilled
and foamy.

4. Strain into the serving glass.

5. Garnish with skewered cocktail cherries.

Jump-Start Me Up

Van Halen: "Jump" + Rolling Stones: "Start Me Up"

¼ to ½ ounce mezcal, to rinse

¾ ounce gin

¾ ounce aromatized white wine

¾ ounce orange liqueur

¾ ounce lemon juice

1 or 2 drops When Doves Cry (page 8)

1 or 2 dashes aromatic bitters

GARNISH

Maraschino cherry

Orange twist

Cocktail skewer

1. Freeze the serving glass for at least 10 to 15 minutes in the freezer.

2. Pour the mezcal into the serving glass and tilt and swirl it around the glass, trying to coat as much of the inside of the glass as possible with the mezcal.

3. Discard or drink the mezcal.

4. In a cocktail shaker filled with ice, add the gin, white wine, orange liqueur, lemon juice, When Doves Cry, and bitters.

5. Shake for 10 to 15 seconds until well chilled.

6. Strain into the mezcal-washed serving glass.

7. Garnish with a skewered cherry and orange twist.

She Works Hard for the Money (All Night Long)

Donna Summer: "She Works Hard for the Money" + Lionel Richie: "All Night Long"

1½ ounces citrus rum

½ ounce lime juice

½ ounce Smooth Operator (page 8)

½ ounce Galliano®, Galliano Vanilla®, or Licor 43®*

3 to 5 dashes orange bitters

Pinch gold luster dust (optional)

2 to 3 ounces prosecco or champagne, chilled

GARNISH

Edible hot pink flower

*Galliano has an anise (licorice-like) flavor, so if you want to dial that down, use Galliano Vanilla or Licor 43 for more of a vanilla flavor.

1. In a cocktail shaker filled with ice, add the rum, lime juice, Smooth Operator, Galliano, bitters, and luster dust (if using).

2. Shake for 10 to 15 seconds until well chilled.

3. Strain into the serving glass.

4. Top with prosecco.

5. Garnish with an edible hot pink flower.

ABOUT THE AUTHORS

CASSANDRA REEDER launched her blog, The Geeky Chef, in 2008, turning fictional food and drinks from a vast array of fandoms into reality with simple and fun recipes. Since then, a series of cookbooks based on the trailblazing blog have been published, including *The Geeky Chef Cookbook* and *The Geeky Bartender Drinks*. In 2023, she released *The Video Game Chef*, a nostalgia-filled culinary adventure featuring iconic foods from video games. In 2024, she co-authored *Lyrics and Libations: The Ultimate '90s Cocktail Playlist*, a spirited tribute to the sweet music of the '90s. When not conjuring up recipes inspired by fiction and pop culture, Cassandra can be found perusing the food carts in Portland, Oregon, with her husband and two tiny agents of chaos.

Thank you to my friend Rob Catalfamo, who at once saved and changed my life with '80s music. I hope you are smiling (and probably also cringing) from wherever you are, Lemonhead.

HENRY BARAJAS is a Latinx author from Tucson, Arizona. He is the co-writer of *The Ultimate '90s Cocktail Playlist* published by Insight Editions. But he is best known in the comic book world for his graphic memoir *La Voz De M.A.Y.O.: Tata Rambo and Helm Greycastle*. Barajas writes *Gil Thorp* for the funny papers in his smoggy Los Angeles, California, home.

Henry would like to dedicate this book to Merwin Yellowhair and Elena Salcedo, and a special thanks to Dan Gibson.

METRIC CONVERSIONS

US	METRIC
⅕ teaspoon (tsp)	1 mL
1 teaspoon (tsp)	5 mL
1 tablespoon (tbsp)	15 mL
1 fluid ounce (fl. oz.)	30 mL
⅕ cup	50 mL
¼ cup	60 mL
⅓ cup	80 mL
3.4 fluid ounces (fl. oz.)	100 mL
½ cup	120 mL
⅔ cup	160 mL
¾ cup	180 mL
1 cup	240 mL
1 pint (2 cups)	480 mL
1 quart (4 cups)	0.95 liter

INSIGHT
EDITIONS

PO Box 3088
San Rafael, CA 94912
www.insighteditions.com

Facebook: www.facebook.com/InsightEditions
Instagram: @insighteditions

ISBN: 979-8-88663-734-2

Publisher: Raoul Goff
VP, Co-Publisher: Vanessa Lopez
Publishing Director: Mike Degler
VP, Creative: Chrissy Kwasnik
VP, Manufacturing: Alix Nicholaeff
Executive Editor: Jennifer Sims
Editorial Assistants: Alecsander Zapata
Managing Editor: Nora Milman
Production Manager: Deena Hashem
Strategic Production Planner: Lina s Palma-Temena

Photography by Waterbury Publications, Inc.

ROOTS of PEACE   REPLANTED PAPER

Insight Editions, in association with Roots of Peace, will plant two trees for each tree used in the manufacturing of this book. Roots of Peace is an internationally renowned humanitarian organization dedicated to eradicating land mines worldwide and converting war-torn lands into productive farms and wildlife habitats. Roots of Peace will plant two million fruit and nut trees in Afghanistan and provide farmers there with the skills and support necessary for sustainable land use.

Manufactured in China by Insight Editions

10 9 8 7 6 5 4 3 2 1